Focus on the Family

Clubhouse

Family Activity Book ™

Focus on the Family Clubhouse Family Activity Book™

edited by Marianne Hering

TYNDALE

Tyndale House Publishers, Wheaton, Illinois

FOCUS ON THE FAMILY CLUBHOUSE FAMILY ACTIVITY BOOK
Copyright 2001 by Focus on the Family.

ISBN: 1-56179-903-3

A Focus on the Family book published by
Tyndale House Publishers, Wheaton, Illinois.

Unless otherwise noted, Scripture quotations are from the *Holy Bible, New International Version* . Copyright 1973, 1978, 1984 by the International Bible Society. Used by permission of Zondervan Publishing House. All rights reserved. Quotations identified KJV are from the King James Version of the Bible.

Cover design by Candi Park D'Agnese and Dale Gehris
Front and back cover illustrations by Dennis Jones
Interior illustrations by Maureen Kimmell

Printed in the United States of America

01 02 03 04 05 06 07 08 09 10/10 9 8 7 6 5 4 3 2 1

Table of Contents

Introduction

If you're like a lot of parents, the last thing you're looking for is more activity. Between driving your children to soccer practice, attending piano recitals, planning birthday parties, fixing meals, and keeping your house from looking like a demilitarized zone, you probably already have enough "activity" in your life.

But chances are when you're about to drop from exhaustion and your brain is stuck in neutral, your kids will hit you with the famous line, "I'm bored." (Maybe you've heard that before?) That's when these fun crafts, activities, and recipes may be exactly what you need. In fact, they're the perfect excuse to keep the TV flipped in the off position and spend some enjoyable time with your children.

From learning about God's creation to playing in the water, from creating righteous orange-juice-can-lid armor to making scrapbooks, these activities will provide hours of entertainment. And best of all, you don't have to be related to Martha Stewart to create a masterpiece. Most everything you need for these ideas can be found around the house and won't cost you a fortune.

For the last 14 years, we've enjoyed dreaming up and printing great activities in *Clubhouse* and *Clubhouse Jr.* magazines. These are some of our favorites. We trust your family will enjoy them and maybe even learn something about God in the process.

God's best,
Jesse Florea, editor of *Clubhouse* magazine

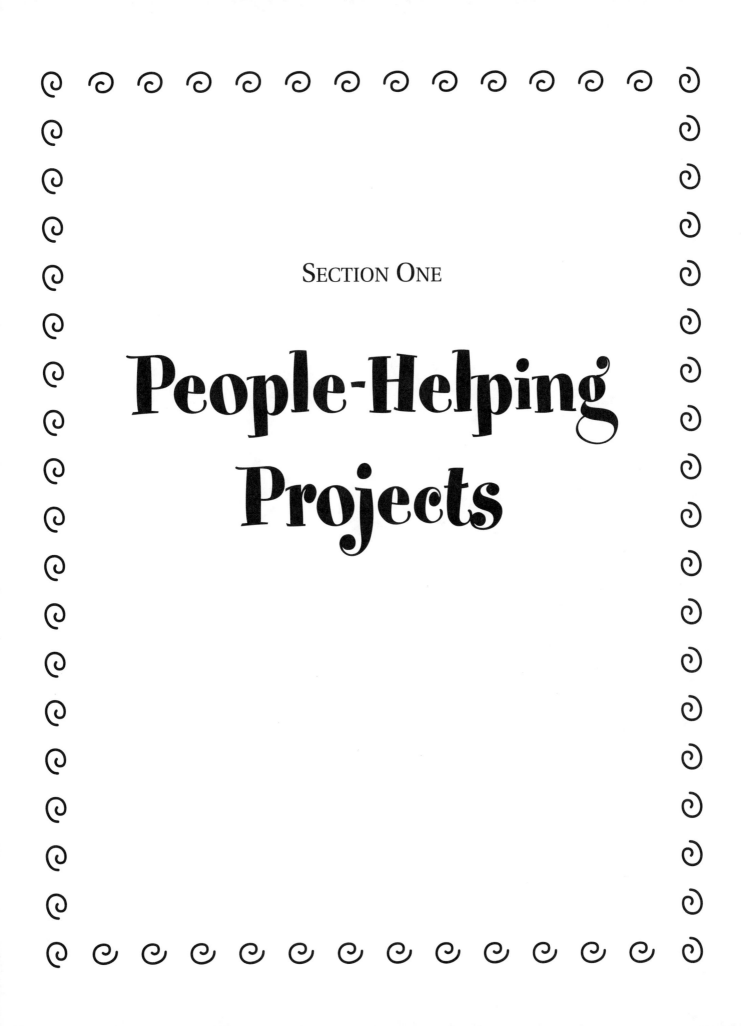

SECTION ONE

People-Helping Projects

1

Serving Coupons

Ages 7 and up

This inexpensive gift will make recipients say, "Thanks a million!"

Gather
- Index cards
- Markers
- Stickers
- Glitter
- Glue
- Other miscellaneous craft supplies
- Stapler

Go
1. Have your child write helpful things he can do on 3x5 index cards.
2. Let him decorate the cards.
3. Help him staple the cards together.
4. Give the cards to Dad for Father's Day, Mom for Mother's Day, or to a neighbor who could use some help.

Grow
Kids need to learn how to serve with a smile. Encourage your child with Philippians 2:14, "Do everything without complaining or arguing," and Colossians 3:23, "Whatever you do, work at it with all your heart, as working for the Lord, not for men."

ɹ ɹ ɹ

2

Faraway Friendships

Ages 6 and up
by Jeanne Gowen Dennis

Here's a way your family can support foreign missionaries.

Gather
- Names of missionaries your church supports
- Information about the missionaries' organizations; for example, in newsletters and books
- Church bulletins

- Local newspaper stories
- Books about each missionary's country

Go

1. Pick one missionary for your family to "adopt." Ask your children to write letters to that missionary each month. Include your Sunday church bulletins and clippings from the local newspaper. As a family, pray for him or her.
2. Read information together each day about the mission's programs and goals. Pray for the work the organization is doing.
3. Read books about the country your missionary lives in. Visit Web sites that have information about the missionary's country.
4. Ask the missionary to find a pen pal from his country for your child to write to and pray for.

Grow

Sometimes our missionaries can seem really far away to our children. As you read about the country your missionary is in, ask your children questions like: "What would you eat if you lived there?" "What kind of house would you most likely have?" "What kinds of activities do the children play there?" "What do you think it is like to go to church there?" Take the regular activities that you do in your home, and put them in the context of the country where the missionary lives.

3

Heart for the Homeless

Ages 7 and up

What would Jesus do for people without homes in your neighborhood?

Gather
- Compassion
- Kindness
- Patience
- Understanding
- Love

Go

These ideas are for the whole family to do together.

1. Use birthday parties or other gatherings as a way of collecting items for the local food bank. For a birthday party scavenger hunt, instead of asking your guests to

find a purple crayon or a green rubber band, give them a list of nonperishable food items to collect. Donate the cans to a food bank.

2. Organize a church, neighborhood, or sports team bake sale. Advertise the sale by passing out fliers or asking teachers and pastors to make announcements. Be sure to tell everyone that the profits will go toward helping a local homeless shelter or food bank.

3. Sort through old toys and books your kids no longer use. Gather up clothes that are too small to wear and put them in bags. Then contact a local shelter to schedule a time to drop off your donation.

4. Organize a concert, play, or other type of performance and donate the admission fees to an organization that helps the homeless. The admission could be cans of food or clean blankets. A church youth group in Michigan rented a high school auditorium and hired several rock groups to play. Since all the proceeds would support the homeless, the Board of Education reduced the rental fee, and the music groups cut their rates, too. The result? Nearly 1,000 people showed up, and the youth group donated $3,700 after expenses. The donation paid for two new apartments for the homeless.

5. Help your kids write to your senators and congressman about the homeless. You can call the local library to find out their names. Share some of your ideas on how to help. Here are the addresses: To The Honorable (name), U.S. Senate, Washington DC 20510. Or To The Honorable (name), U.S. House of Representatives, Washington, DC 20515.

6. Prepare food with your family or church group to bring to a center for the homeless. Youth groups in Minnesota and Massachusetts bake cupcakes and drop them off in the afternoon at local shelters. Once a week, girls in a Connecticut Brownie troop prepare dinner for 45 shelter residents.

7. Go as a family to play with kids who live at a shelter. Bring along crafts or games to share with residents. You can bring neighborhood friends along, too.

8. Work directly with those who are homeless by volunteering at a shelter or food pantry. You can always help with serving meals, but there is also behind-the-scenes work that needs to be done. Offer to file papers, sort clothes, restock shelves, bag groceries, etc. Think about what your children do best and then call a few places in your area to offer your talents.

9. Make a "homeless bag." Gather pop-top cans of food, granola bars, beef jerky, and Christian tracts. Put all the stuff into plastic bags and keep them in your car. Pass them out to the homeless people you see while you're driving.—*Christopher Milligan*

Before undertaking any homeless project, be sure your children follow these guidelines:
- Go with an adult friend or family member to the shelters or areas where homeless people live.
- Never give cash to a homeless person. Instead buy the person a sandwich, a needed piece of clothing, or a personal hygiene product.
- Speak with respect to the person.
- Be neighborly and think about how Jesus would treat that person. Realize that homeless people are not all the same.
- Share God's love and His Word when you can.

Grow

Seeing the problems of the poor can be stressful and frightening. Keep close tabs on your children's feelings and emotional well-being while undertaking any service project with the homeless. Your family can't solve all the world's problems, but God can. Pray for the homeless every day—it's not just lip service.

ℯ   ℯ   ℯ

4

Pennies from Heaven

Ages 4 and up
adapted from a story by Jan Merop

This helping project uses "common cents" to provide inexpensive gifts for nursing home patients, college freshmen, or a homeless shelter.

Gather
- Large jar
- Coins (from family, friends, neighbors, under the couch, between the car seats, or anywhere else stray coins wind up)

Go
1. As a family, make a goal to save up money all summer. Give up a trip to the swimming pool or ice cream parlor and let your children put the money in a jar. Encourage them to do extra chores and put the money they would have earned in the jar. Help older children get jobs outside the house, like mowing a neighbor's lawn, and make a donation to the jar. (For more ideas, see "The Buck Starts Here" on page 83.)
2. Next, choose a charity, person, or group of people who could use some small, inexpensive gifts and cheerful notes. It could be a homeless shelter (toothpaste, deodorant), a nursing home (lemon drops, candles), a freshman dorm (quarters for laundry and vending machines, powdered laundry soap in plastic bags, stationery items, stamps, candy bars), or a group of hurricane victims (they need everything!). Begin to pray for the people you choose.
3. Take the money out of the jar and count it. Talk about appropriate gifts to give to the people, make a budget, and go purchase gifts.
4. Help your children wrap the gifts and write encouraging notes with Bible verses attached.
5. Deliver the gifts in person, if possible.

Grow

After you are all finished with the project, resist the urge to reward your children with a special treat or outing. Let kindness and the Lord's approval be reward enough. Read Colossians 3:17 together: "And whatever you do, whether in word or deed, do it all in the name of the Lord Jesus, giving thanks to God the Father through him," and make it your family summer motto.

ℰ ℰ ℰ

5

Big, Bad Trash Attack

Ages 4 and up
by Charlotte Adelsperger

Clean up your park, neighborhood, or camping area with this grime-fighting game.

Gather
- Your children and their friends
- 4 or more large garbage bags
- Whistle

Go
1. Divide the children into teams of two or three.
2. Give each team two bags (one for trash and the other for recyclable items).
3. Explain the rules: Each piece of trash is worth two points and every recyclable item is worth three points. No trash picked out of a garbage can or trash bin will count. It's against the rules to tear up trash into smaller pieces in order to get more points.
4. The players have 30 minutes to pick up the trash lying on the ground. When you blow the whistle, time is up and everyone must return to the starting spot. (With younger children, you will want to spend less time and restrict the size of the area where they are collecting trash so that you can supervise more closely.)
5. Count everyone's collection and name the winning team. Don't forget to throw away the trash and sort the recyclable items. Then take the items to be recycled.

Grow

Make sure all the players feel like a winner because everyone "wins" when the neighborhood looks good. Point out that this is a way to keep God's creation looking good, not only for them but also for the others who live in the neighborhood or use the park or camping area.

ℰ   ℰ   ℰ

6

People Pleasers

Ages 6 and up

Here are eight quick ways to show friends, family, and neighbors you care.

1. Put a child in the "hot seat" surrounded by a circle of friends or family members who take turns saying something nice about him.
2. Write verses from Proverbs on slips of paper. Place them in the middle of chocolate sandwich cookies so the paper sticks out. Serve to your child's friends.
3. August 1 is Friendship Day. Let your child call a friend and invite him or her to a church activity or to your home to watch a Christian video.
4. Make a heart-shaped card for grandparents.
5. Write a fun letter. Include stickers, sticks of gum, pictures, and your favorite Bible verse. Mail it to someone who could use some cheering up.
6. Buy a box of plain adhesive bandage strips. Write portions of verses about being saved or mending a relationship with God. Some you might use are Psalm 147:3, Jonah 2:9, John 3:16, Ephesians 2:8. Let your child give the bandages away to friends.
7. Fill a plastic bag with gummy worms. Write the words about being "fishers of men" (Matthew 4:18-20) on a card and put it in the bag also. Give it to a friend your child wants "hooked" on Christ.
8. Let your child draw a sheep on the blank side of an index card. On the other side, write Psalm 100:3 or another verse about sheep following the Shepherd. Then cut up the index card like puzzle pieces and let your child send it to a friend. Be sure your child follows up and asks the recipient if she'd like to know more about Jesus.

Grow
It's good for our children to have ways to encourage their friends. Spend time talking with your children about whom God might want them to share their faith with. How can they follow up after giving them a token that represents God's love for them?

SECTION TWO

Games–
Indoors

7

Cowboy Checkers

Ages 7 and up

Your kids will "jump" right into this Western game with three variations.

A bandanna and some spare change turn into an on-the-go checker game.

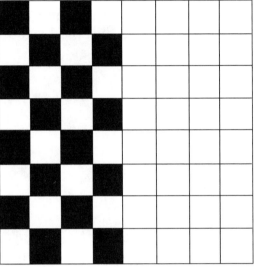

Gather
- Bandanna
- Black permanent marker
- Masking tape
- Ruler
- 12 nickels and 12 pennies

Go
You'll have to make this for younger kids (7-9). Older kids (10 and up) can make it for themselves.
1. Find the center of the bandanna by folding it in half, then in half again. Make a small dot in the center.
2. Tape the bandanna to a flat surface covered with newspaper or cardboard to protect against marker stains.
3. Place a ruler on the center mark. Draw a line from one edge of the plain center section of the bandanna to the other, parallel to the edge of the cloth. Draw quickly so the ink won't spread.
4. Draw another line from edge to edge through the center dot, perpendicular to the first line. (The lines should form a cross.)
5. Draw three lines, $1^1/_4$ inches apart, on each side of the first center line. Turn the bandanna and do the same with the other center line.
6. Draw lines around the outside of the checkerboard.
7. Blacken every other square.
8. Your child can carry the coins (or checkers if he has some) wherever he goes by wrapping them in the bandanna board. One player is heads, and the other is tails.

Fox and Geese

Ages 7 and up

Gather
- Checkerboard
- Checkers
- Two players

13

Go

1. One player places the red checkers on the board as you would for a regular game. These are the geese. They cannot make jumps.
2. The other player puts one black checker, called the fox, in the opposite corner.
3. Players can move only on the dark squares, one square at a time.
4. The fox goes first. The fox can jump, and it can make multiple jumps in one turn. Jumped geese are removed from the board.
5. The object of the game for the fox is to reach the last row on the other side of the board without being captured by the geese.
6. For the geese, the object is to surround the fox so it can't move.

Checker Solitaire

Ages 7 and up

Gather
- Checkerboard
- Checkers

Go

1. The player tries to place eight checkers on eight squares so that no two pieces are in the same row, column or diagonal. (The example is only one of many ways to win.)

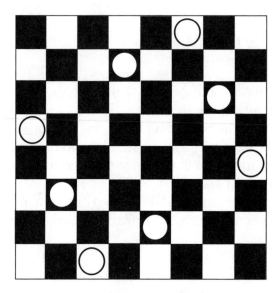

Five in a Row

Ages 7 and up

Gather
- 2 players
- Checkers
- Checkerboard

Go

1. Each player picks a checker color.
2. Players take turns placing one checker at a time on the board anywhere they like.
3. Players take turns moving the checkers one square in any direction; no jumping allowed.

4. Whenever one player has five checkers in a row, he may remove one of the other player's checkers from the board. Each player tries to block his opponent from getting five in a row.
5. The player with only four checkers left on the board loses.

Grow

Since checkers is a popular game with "kids" of all ages, this would be a great way for your child to reach out to seniors in your neighborhood or church. Make a list of all the seniors your child knows, and ask him to challenge one to a game.

8

Marble Mania

These eight great games are a "sure shot" to capture your kids' enthusiasm.

The Playing Ring
Ages 6 and up

Gather
- 20 or so regular marbles
- Shooter marble for each player
- Chalk
- Shoe (for the game "Puggy")
- Shoe box (for the game "Boxies")
- Two or more children

Go
To make sure the game is set up well, create the playing ring for your children. Older children can watch the first time and play on their own afterward.

1. To set up the games, draw a big chalk playing ring at least 12 inches in diameter. Smooth concrete or hardwood floors work well for the playing area.
2. Draw two straight lines on opposite sides of the circle. The lines should be parallel and 1 inch away from the circle.

3. Teach your child how to shoot a marble. He places the knuckle of his first finger on the cement. He holds the shooter marble between his first finger and his thumb. Then he flicks his thumb, spinning the marble slowly into the ring.
4. Have him practice until he has confidence. If it is too difficult or you have a very young child, skip the first four games and try "Handy Dandy," "Boxies" or "Groundhog."

Traditional Marbles

Ages 6 and up

Go

1. To see who goes first, have each player put one marble on the same line. Each player shoots his marble, hoping it will stop close to the opposite, parallel line. The player whose marble comes closest to the line without going past it goes first.
2. Each player places three marbles in the ring. These marbles are called "ante."
3. The first player shoots his "shooter" from anywhere outside the ring. He is trying to knock one of the other player's marbles out of the ring. If he does so, he captures the marble, now called a "duck," and puts it in a pile called his "victory pile." If he captures a duck, he goes again. If he does not, it is the next player's turn.
4. The play continues until all the marbles are out of the circle. (Shooters are removed from the circle after each turn.) The winner is the person with the most marbles in his victory pile.

Dead Ducks

Ages 6 and up

Go

1. Each player places three marbles on one of the straight lines. These are the "ducks."
2. Players take turns shooting at the ducks from the other line with a shooter marble.
3. If a player knocks one of the ducks off the line, she puts it in her victory pile.
4. If she misses, she adds another one of her marbles (duck) to the line, and the next player shoots.
5. The game ends when all the ducks have been knocked off the line.
6. The winner is the player with the most ducks in her victory pile.

Tic-Tac-Toe

Ages 6 and up

Go

For two players:
1. With the chalk, draw a tic-tac-toe board with 6-inch squares on the playing area.
2. Draw a shooting line about three feet away.
3. Each player tries to get three of his marbles in a row on the board.

4. The first player shoots his marble, trying to get it to land inside a tic-tac-toe square.
5. The players alternate shooting one marble at a time, trying to get a marble to land in a square or to knock the opponent's marble out of a square.
6. The first person to land on a square has control unless his marble is knocked out and the other player has a marble inside the square.
7. The play continues until a player has tic-tac-toe.

Puggy

Ages 6 and up

Go

1. One of the players removes her shoe and places it in the middle of the playing ring.
2. Each player drops three or four marbles into the ring.
3. The first player aims her shooter at one of the marbles in the ring and tries to make that marble hit the shoe.
4. If she does, she puts the marble in her victory pile and shoots again.
5. If she fails, the next player shoots.
6. The game is over when all the target marbles have been captured.
7. The winner has the most marbles in her victory pile.

Handy Dandy

Ages 6 and up

Go

1. Each player starts with the same amount of marbles.
2. One player puts some marbles in his hand and holds up his closed fist.
3. The other player tries to guess how many marbles he is holding.
4. If he's right, he wins all the marbles.
5. If he's wrong, he must "pay" the first player the difference between the number he guessed and the actual number of marbles.
6. After each player has had an equal number of turns, the winner is the player with the most marbles.
7. If there is a tie, hold a play-off hand between the winners.

Boxies

Ages 4 and up

Go

1. Set a shoe box on its side with the opening toward the players.
2. The players take four big steps backward.
3. Players take turns rolling their marbles toward the box, trying to get them to stay inside.
4. The marbles must stay inside the box. If the marble rolls out, it doesn't count.
5. The winner is the one with the most marbles in the box.

Groundhog

Ages 4 and up

Go

This game is played on hard-packed dirt.
1. Dig a small hole and draw a line about three feet away.
2. Each player tosses her marbles toward the "hog's hole" from the line.
3. The first player to get three marbles in the hole wins.

Ducks in the Pond

Ages 6 and up

Go

This game uses the same playing area as "Groundhog."
1. Each player drops three marbles onto the dirt near the hole.
2. Beginning at the line, the first player shoots at the marbles (ducks), trying to knock one into the hole (pond).
3. If he hits one of the ducks (whether it goes into the pond or not), he tries again from where his shooter stopped.
4. If he misses, the next player takes a turn.
5. The game is over when all the ducks are in the pond, and the winner is the person who knocked in the most ducks.

Grow

If your child loved these marbles games, have him host a "Lose Your Marbles" party and invite new neighbors over to play.

SECTION THREE

Games–
Outdoors

9

Moccasin Medley

Enjoy these five games that American Indian children played.

Hide and Hoot

Ages 6 and up

Gather
- 4 or more children
- Whistle

Go
1. Find an area with lots of hiding places such as a treed park, the woods, or a treed section of your neighborhood. Set boundaries so players don't run too far.
2. Pick one child to be chief, and give that player a whistle.
3. While the chief counts to 50 (or less for younger children), everybody tries to find a good hiding place.
4. When the chief finishes counting, he lets out a loud hoot and everybody must freeze. The chief gets three minutes (or less for younger children) to find everybody. At the end of the time, the chief blows the whistle and the players return to the starting spot.
5. The players who weren't spotted earn a point, and a new chief is picked. Once everybody has been the chief, the player with the most points is the victor.

Choose Which Cup

Ages 6 and up

Gather
- 4 plastic foam cups
- Ball
- 2 children

Go
1. Place the cups side by side on a table.
2. One person hides the ball under one of the cups while the other player is not looking.
3. If the guesser finds the ball on her first try, she scores 20 points. If it takes her two guesses, give her 15. Three guesses will get her 10, while four guesses earns just five points.
4. Once she's guessed correctly, have her hide the ball for the other child.
5. The first player to score 100 wins.

Tripod Tag

Ages 6 and up

Gather
- 6 children minimum; even numbers work best
- Long strips of cloth

Go
1. Have everybody choose a buddy.
2. Give each pair a strip of cloth. Use the cloth to tie one ankle of each pair together.
3. Decide which pair is going to be "it."
4. Ask all of the teams to spread out, and then start the game of three-legged tag.

Kick the Stick

Ages 6 and up

Gather
- $^3/_4$-inch dowel rod
- Friends
- Markers
- Yarn or ribbon

Go
1. Saw the dowel into 5-inch sections.
2. Give each player one piece of the rod and have her decorate it with the markers, yarn, or ribbon.
3. Go outside and lay the sticks on the grass in a straight line about three feet apart.
4. Decide how far the players will race—to the end of the yard or to a fire hydrant, for example.
5. Ask each player to stand behind her stick.
6. Shout, "Go!"
7. The first person to kick her stick past the finish line is the winner.

Pick the Pattern

Ages 7 and up

Gather
- File folder
- Scissors
- Markers
- Notebook paper
- 2 children

Go

1. Cut out 20 shapes from the folder. Cut squares, triangles, rectangles, and circles. Have some match and some be one-of-a-kind.
2. Let your child design and color some with dots, some with stripes, and some solids. The object is to create some identical-looking shapes and some different-looking ones.
3. Pick one person to be chief.
4. The other person turns her back as the chief arranges the shapes in a pattern. The chief draws the pattern or writes a description of the pattern on the piece of paper and asks the other person to turn around.
5. The contestant studies the pattern for one or two minutes. Then the chief gathers all of the shapes, mixes them up and asks the contestant to recreate the pattern.
6. Once she has made her guess, the chief checks the answer and the two switch roles.
7. Start with a pattern of seven shapes and see how many more your child can add.

Grow

Most American Indian games were not played just for fun, but for building survival skills. For example, "Hide and Hoot" taught them how to be quiet in the wilderness. As your children play these games, encourage them to work on building spiritual skills. Learning how to lose—and win—with grace needs to be practiced. Here are a list of verses to discuss with your children: Jeremiah 9:23-24, Matthew 20:26-28, 1 Corinthians 13:4-5.

10

Wet 'n' Wild

Make a big splash with these 11 water games.

Balloon Burst

Ages 4 and up

This tossing game is aloft with thrills.

Gather
- Your children and their friends
- Water balloons

Go

1. Match everybody with a partner. The pairs stand two steps apart and face each other.
2. One of the partners takes a water balloon and tosses it to her friend. If she catches it, she takes a giant step backward and throws it back. If she misses, and the balloon doesn't break, she stays where she is and tosses the balloon back.

3. Whenever a player catches the balloon, she takes a step backward. The pair keeps playing catch until the balloon pops.
4. The winning team is the pair who ends up the farthest away from each other.

Water Piñata

Ages 4 and up

Turn a water balloon into a water piñata.

Gather
  • Large water balloon
  • Blindfold
  • Stick

Go
  1. Fill a large water balloon.
  2. Hang it from a branch or a pole.
  3. Blindfold a player and give him a stick.
  4. Spin him around a few times until he's a tad dizzy.
  5. See if he can hit the balloon in three swings; if not, the next player takes a turn.
  6. The winner wins a nice, cool shower.

Buckets of Fun

Ages 4 and up

This fast-paced race relays excitement.

Gather
  • Bucket for each player or teams of players, plus one extra bucket
  • Plastic cups

Go
  1. Fill the largest bucket with water and put it at one end of the yard. Keep the hose handy in case it runs out of water.
  2. For each team/player, put an empty bucket at the other end of the yard.
  3. Give each child one or two plastic cups.
  4. At the "go" signal, each child will race to the full bucket, fill the cups, and carry them back to the empty buckets. After pouring the cups into the bucket, the child races to fill the bucket to the brim. Any spills will water the lawn.

Hide and Squirt

Ages 4 and up

This variation of a familiar game is streaming with fun.

Gather
- Friends
- Spray bottle or squirt gun

Go
1. Decide who is going to be "it." Give that child the spray bottle.
2. While everybody else hides, the child with the water bottle covers his eyes and counts to 25.
3. When "it" is done counting, he looks for each player.
4. To catch the other players, he squirts them. The last player to get caught becomes "it," and the next round starts.

Meltdown

Ages 4 and up
by Sarah Yoder

Your kids will dissolve into laughter as they race to melt an ice cube.

Gather
- 2 children minimum
- Ice cube for each player

Go
1. If players have on long-sleeved shirts or pants, have them change into shorts and T-shirts.
2. Give each player an ice cube approximately the same size.
3. Each player must try to melt the ice cube as quickly as possible by rubbing it against his skin. Players cannot put the ice cubes in their mouths.
4. The first player who melts the ice cube completely is the winner.

Paint the Town

Ages 4 and up

Add a few strokes of fun with this simple water activity.

Gather
- Buckets
- Large paintbrush for each child

Go

1. Fill each bucket with water.
2. Give the kids a paintbrush and let them "paint" the fence, house, deck, or garage door with water.

Presto Rainbow

Ages 4 and up

This arc of water creates a burst of color.

Gather

- Sunny afternoon
- Garden hose

Go

1. Have your child stand so that the sun is behind her.
2. Take the hose and spray a fine mist just above and in front of her.
3. Ask her to look into the spray and watch for a rainbow.

Soda-Bottle Shower

Ages 4 and up

This simple sprinkler will leave kids dripping with giggles.

Gather

- Empty plastic soda bottle
- Scissors, small screwdriver, or craft knife

Go

1. Poke about 20 holes in the bottom of the soda bottle.
2. Go outside and fill it with water.
3. Let the water sprinkle all over the kids.
4. Take it on camping trips for quick cleanups or use it to water delicate outdoor plants.

Squirt Squad

Ages 4 and up

Kids will have a blast at this backyard "shooting" gallery.

Gather
- Squirt gun or spray bottle for each child
- 10 plastic cups, minimum

Go
1. Outside on a bench or table, stack the 10 empty cups in a pyramid. (Four on the bottom row, three on top of that, etc.)
2. Give each child a full squirt gun and position him about 3 feet away from the cups.
3. At the "go" signal, see how fast he can shoot down the cups.
4. If there are two or more kids, gather more cups and stage a race.

Water Pistol Picasso

Ages 4 and up

"Watercolor" takes on a whole new meaning with this outdoor art gallery.

Gather
- Squirt gun or a clean empty spray bottle
- Food coloring
- Masking tape, duct tape, or tacks
- Big sheets of butcher paper or newsprint

Go
1. Tape or tack up a sheet of paper to the fence or sidewalk.
2. Fill the squirt gun or bottle with water. Add a few drops of food coloring and shake well.
3. Let your child squirt some fun designs on the paper.
4. Change water and colors frequently.
5. Let the colors dry in the sun before bringing them inside.

Water Snake

Ages 4 and up

Whip up some fun with this simple hose trick.

Gather
- Strong wooden stake or post
- Wire or strong strips of fabric

- Garden hose with high-pressure nozzle (plastic works best)
- Children who want to get wet

Go

1. Find an open, grassy area and firmly plant the stake in the ground.
2. Leaving about three feet at the end, tie the hose to the stake.
3. Turn on the water, adjusting the hose length and water pressure until the hose is wriggling and squirting all over.
4. Turn the children loose.

Grow

Water is key to life, and in the summer, it is key to fun, too. Turn to page 40 and do the activities in "Wacky, Wonderful Water." Your kids will discover why water is one of God's spectacular creations.

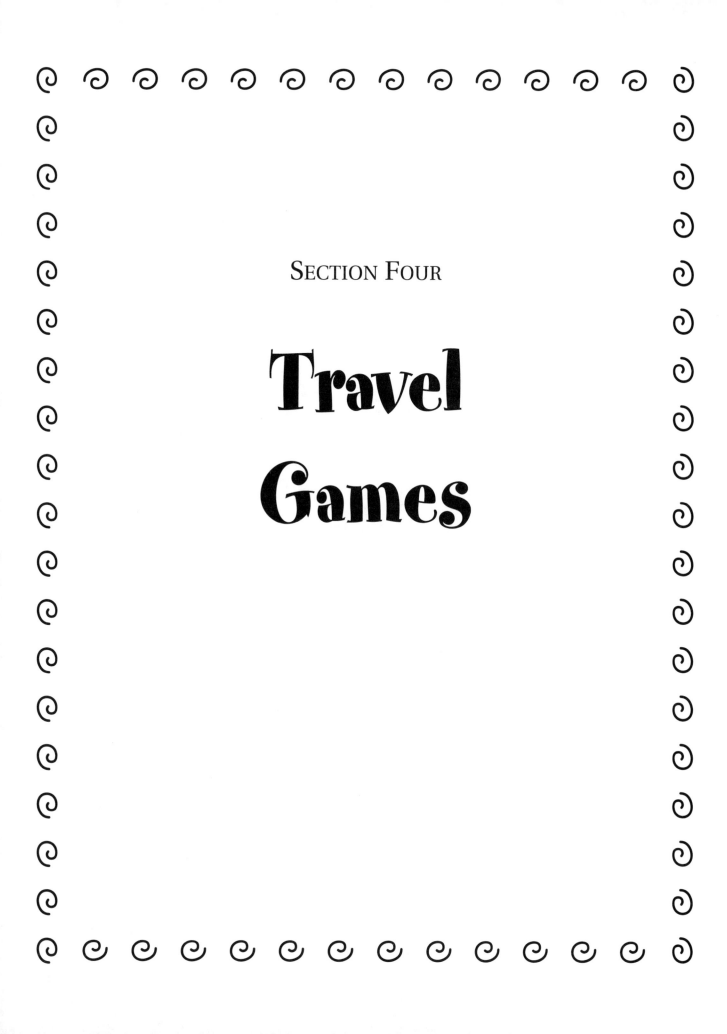

SECTION FOUR

Travel
Games

11

On the Move

Whether your family is driving, hiking, or flying, these games make the journey more fun.

Alphabeticalifornia!

Ages 5 and up

This game is as simple as A-B-C.

Go
1. Think of something that starts with the letter *a*, such as an apple.
2. Use that object in a sentence that begins, "I'm going to California (or wherever), and I'm taking an apple."
3. The next person repeats the phrase and adds a *b* word. "I'm going to California and I'm taking an apple and a banjo."
4. The next person adds a *c* word and so on until someone makes a mistake.
5. Got a group of older children? Ask them to begin with *z* and work backward.

Bloodhound

Ages 4 and up

By looking through old magazines, your kids will be on the hunt for fun.

Gather
• Old magazines with lots of pictures

Go
1. Give your child an old magazine.
2. Call out a letter and let your child find a picture that begins with that letter. For example, if you say *h*, your child finds a hamburger. If your child does not know how to spell, stay away from words that begin with sounds that could be represented by more than one letter, such as *s*, *c*, and *k*.
3. If you want to extend the time your child spends on the task, set a time limit of about three minutes and see how many items he can find.

Bump Pictures

Ages 4 and up

In for a rocky ride? This drawing game turns every jostle into a masterpiece.

Gather
- Paper
- Sturdy book to write on
- Sharp pencil
- Markers or crayons

Go
1. Let your child hold the book as a makeshift desk. Put the paper on top of the book in the passenger's lap.
2. Your child holds the pencil with the tip on the paper, letting the bumps of the car move it.
3. After a while, look at what your child has drawn and brainstorm what it could be.
4. Let him color in the picture with markers or crayons.

Drawing Duel

Ages 6 and up

Want to stop backseat bickering? Invite your kids to end their squabbles with a showdown using this "quick draw" technique.

Gather
- Paper
- Pencil
- Die
- Shoe box lid

Go

Each child will draw a portion of a picture after she rolls the correct number on the die. The first player to complete the picture is the winner. Got a child riding alone? Turn this game into a solo sketching session.
1. Players take turns trying to roll a "one."
2. The first player to roll a "one" sketches the portion of the drawing in box number one. Her turn is then ended.
3. The next player rolls. If she rolls a "one," she then sketches what is in box number one. If she does not roll a "one," it is the next player's turn.

4. Players keep taking turns tossing the die until they roll the next number in the sequence to finish their picture.
5. If a player does not roll the next number in her sequence, her turn is skipped.
6. The play continues until a player finishes her picture.
7. When your kids finish with this picture, make up some of your own.

Jan Ken Pon

Ages 4 and up

This Oriental version of "Rock, Paper, Scissors" is a sure bet to delight your children.

Go
1. Each player makes a fist with one hand and moves it up and down saying *jan ken pon*. (*Jan* means tweezers in Japanese and scissors in Chinese; *ken* means rock or fist in Japanese; *pon* means wrap or paper in Chinese.)
2. After the third upward movement, each player brings his fist down and makes one of three symbols: first and middle fingers extended = scissors; a fist = a rock; a flat hand palm upward = paper.
3. Rock beats scissors; scissors beats paper; paper beats rock.
4. If both players choose the same thing, they repeat the steps listed above, this time saying *Ai kode sho* (both are the same).
5. When one person wins, he says *kachi mashita* (winner) and then *atchi mite hoi* (look the other way). He then points to the right or left.
6. The other player tries to guess which way he will point by turning his head in the opposite direction. Then the opponents play again.

On-the-Go Bingo

Ages 6 and up

Create game boards to keep in the car for long trips or to liven up a routine ride.

Gather
- Square sheet of white paper for each player
- Markers or colored pencils
- Stickers (optional)
- Con-Tact paper

Go
Ask older kids to create their own bingo cards during the trip. Younger children will need you to prepare their cards ahead of time.
1. By cutting 2$^{1}/_{2}$ inches off the length of an 8$^{1}/_{2}$-by-11-inch sheet of paper, create a square card for each player.
2. Draw a grid on each sheet with at least 16 boxes.

3. In each square, draw something your children are likely to see from the road such as a horse, a bicycle, or a police car. Other options: use stickers or print words. If you are going on foot, draw pictures or use stickers of plants, rock formations, outhouses, etc.
4. Arrange the items differently on each card, and make sure each paper has a few unique drawings.
5. Cover each card with clear Con-Tact paper.
6. To play, mark the proper square as you see each item on the sheet.
7. The first person to mark all the squares in a row either diagonally, across, up, or down wins.
8. A grand-prize winner is anyone who marks off every square.

Windy Weather

Ages 4 and up

This travel game appeals to children who like to keep their eyes peeled.

Go
1. Keep your eyes open for a windmill, weather vane, or a flag waving in the breeze.
2. The player who firsts spots the object earns 10 points.
3. Begin the game again when someone reaches 100 points.

Grow
Your children can also use their travel time wisely by memorizing Scripture. See "Word Games" on page 43 for some great techniques.

SECTION FIVE

Learn with Love and Laughter– Indoor Activities

12

Common Senses

Music to Your Ears

Ages 4 and up

Gather
- 4 identical drinking glasses
- Water
- Spoon

Go
1. Fill the glasses with different amounts of water, about $1/4$, $1/2$, $3/4$, and full.
2. Let your child gently tap the side of each glass near the top. Can she hear the different tones?
3. What did your child discover? The more water, the lower/higher the tone.

Fun Fact: Your smallest bones aren't in your pinkie fingers or baby toes. You have three teeny-tiny bones inside each ear.

Color Mixing

Ages 4 and up

Gather
- White paper
- Markers

Go
1. With a yellow marker, draw a circle about the size of a golf ball on one side of the paper.
2. Color in the circle.
3. Let your child stare at the circle and slowly count to 40. (Hint: Don't let him move his eyes too much.)
4. Have him quickly look at the blank side of the white paper. Does he see a spot? Ask him what color it is. (It should be red.)
5. Try the same thing with red, purple, and blue circles. What are the colors of their after-images?

Fun Fact: Even though you can see only the front of your eye, your eyeball is actually about the size of a Ping-Pong ball.

Swell Smell

Ages 4 and up

Gather
- Cinnamon
- Cough medicine
- Dill pickles
- Mint leaves
- Onion
- Small opaque cups
- Aluminum foil
- Sharp pencil

Go

Upper-elementary-aged children can do the setup on their own. Younger ones will need your help throughout.
1. Put each smelly item in its own cup.
2. Cover the cups with foil. Carefully poke small holes in the foil with a pencil. Make sure the cups are numbered.
3. Invite your child to close his eyes and use his sniffer to figure out what is in each cup. Write his guesses on a piece of paper.
4. Uncover the cups. Compare what's in the cups to the guesses.
5. Close your eyes and let your child offer you the cups. Write down your guesses.
6. When everyone has had a turn, start the guessing game over with different smells in new cups.

Fun Fact: Your nose is better at figuring out flavor than your tongue. The scent it picks up helps your brain know what you're eating.

Touchy Subject

Ages 4 and up

Gather
- Emery board
- Metal nail file
- Grape
- Peeled grape
- Small, dry sponge
- Small, wet sponge
- Lemon
- Orange
- 2 screwdrivers that are similar in size but not identical

Go

1. Spread out the items on a table in front of your child.
2. Ask her to close her eyes and hold out her hands.
3. Pick one of the items from the table and put it in her hands. When she is done feeling it, take it from her and place it on the table in its original spot.
4. Have her open her eyes. Can she pick out what she felt?
5. When you've gone through everything, switch places and use different items.

Fun Fact: You have about 100 touch receptors on the tip of each finger that help you feel temperature and pain.

Tricky Taste Buds

Ages 4 and up

Gather

- Bite-sized chunk of apple
- Hunk of fresh onion
- Blindfold

Go

1. Blindfold your child.
2. Carefully hold the onion close to his nose while feeding him the apple.
3. Can he guess what he tasted?

Fun Fact: Your tongue's 3000 taste buds figure out if food is salty, sweet, sour, or bitter. But a dry tongue can't taste anything.

Grow

Ask your child what his favorite sense is and why. Ask him what it would be like to not have one of his senses. Then read aloud 1 Corinthians 12:14-20:

> Now the body is not made up of one part, but of many. If the foot should say, "Because I am not a hand, I do not belong to the body," it would not for that reason cease to be part of the body. And if the ear should say, "Because I am not an eye, I do not belong to the body," it would not for that reason cease to be part of the body. If the whole body were an eye, where would the sense of hearing be? If the whole body were an ear, where would the sense of smell be? But in fact God has arranged the parts in the body, every one of them, just as he wanted them to be. If they were all one part, where would the body be? As it is, there are many parts, but one body.

Ask your child what role he has in your family. Assure him that just as all the senses have a unique and useful role, he is a wanted and needed part of your family and God's family.

e e e

13

Wacky, Wonderful Water

by Jeanne Gowen Dennis

God made water on the second day of creation. Learn more about water—and God—by doing these experiments that are soaking in fun.

Rising to the Challenge
Ages 6 and up

Water can travel uphill.

Gather
- Pencil or awl
- 2 clear plastic cups
- Soil
- Pebbles or marbles

Go
1. With a pencil or an awl, punch a few small holes in the bottom of two clear plastic cups.
2. Let your child fill one cup with dry soil and the other with pebbles or marbles.
3. She should place the cups in bowls filled with $1/2$ cup of water each.
4. Help her check the experiment after an hour. The water should have risen into the soil several inches. The water in the other cup should be about the same level as the water in the bowl.

What causes these results? It's called capillary action, a force that defies gravity. Water molecules will flow up extremely narrow tubes, such as the tiny spaces between soil particles. Spaces between the pebbles or marbles in the other cup are too large for capillary action to work, so the water doesn't rise as high.

Grow
It seems impossible for water to go upward, just as it seems impossible for us to forgive someone who has hurt us. Remind your child that God has designed creation so that nothing is impossible if she relies on Him.

Going, Going, Gone

Ages 6 and up

Water can vanish into thin air—and come right back in a flash.

Gather
- Water
- Saucer
- A warm day
- Empty glass/metal cup
- Freezer

Go
1. Put one tablespoon of water onto a saucer.
2. Leave it uncovered in a warm or sunny spot. Eventually, the water will evaporate, change to a gas (water vapor), and become part of the air.
3. Place an empty glass or metal cup in the freezer. Remove it after 15 minutes.
4. When warm air hits the cold cup, water vapor from the air will condense on the cup, changing from vapor to frost and then to liquid water.

Grow
When things are going badly, it might seem that God has disappeared from our lives. Remind your child that even though he can't see God, He's always there to help.

Hide and Seek

Ages 6 and up

Water masks other substances.

Gather
- Sugar
- Drinking Glass
- Water

Go
1. Let your child stir a tablespoon of sugar into a cup of water until the sugar disappears.
2. Have him taste the water. It's sweet, even though it still looks clear. The water is carrying the sugar in solution.

Many solids, liquids, and gases can be either dissolved or suspended (carried) in water. This is one reason it isn't safe to drink water from a pool, lake, or stream, even if it looks clean. Water can harbor harmful substances that can't be seen.

Grow
Teach your child that Jesus washes our sins away by carrying them Himself. He takes away all the harmful things we've done or said and dissolves them into a sea of forgiveness.

Wet All Over

Ages 6 and up

Use a zucchini to show that water hides in living things.

Gather
- Bowl
- Cucumber or zucchini
- Salt

Go
1. In a bowl, mix some slices of cucumber or zucchini with salt.
2. After several minutes, water will flow out of the vegetables into the bowl. If too much water leaves the cells of the vegetable, the cells will shrivel up and die.

Grow

As the Living Water, Jesus gives us eternal life and quenches our thirst for love forever.

Safe and Sound

Ages 6 and up

Icy water can keep things warm!

Gather
- Grapes
- 2 plastic bowls
- Water

Go
1. Put some grapes into a plastic bowl. Cover them with at least three inches of water and put them into the freezer.
2. Freeze a few other grapes in a bowl or cup without water.
3. Check the grapes every 20 minutes.
4. When there is a layer of ice on the water that does not break when you touch it, take all the grapes from the freezer.
5. Remove the layer of ice from the bowl. The grapes in the water should be fine. The unprotected grapes will be frozen, turning mushy and brown as they thaw. Water loses and gains heat slowly. Ice layered over a lake helps keep the fish from freezing in winter.

Grow

Sometimes it may seem to your child that obeying God's laws will keep her from having fun. Remind her that God's rules are like a covering, protecting her from harm.

14

Word Games

Ages 5 and up
by Erin Fisk

Here are some favorite tried-and-true ways to memorize a verse.

Gather
- Note cards
- Paper
- Chalkboard or whiteboard

Go
1. Write the verse down on a card and hang it up where your child spends a lot of time. You could put it in the bathroom, and when your child brushes his teeth he can say it to himself several times.
2. Make a memory puzzle. Write his verse on a piece of paper and cut it up. Can he put it back together? This can help kids who are learning how to read memorize the verse.
3. With the verse written on a chalkboard, erase one word at a time. See if he can remember the erased word.
4. Write down the verse and put a different symbol next to each word. To have your child remember it, just ask him to remember the symbols. Younger children can do this with you even if they can't read.

Grow
Most of the verses your child will be asked to memorize come from a Sunday school lesson or Bible club meetings. When memorizing at home, ask your child what type of verse he wants to memorize. He may choose a short one like John 11:35, "Jesus wept." But more likely he'll delightfully surprise you and pick a verse with special spiritual importance to him.

Learn with Love and Laughter– Outdoor Activities

15

Grave Celebration

Ages 8 and up
by Genetta Adair

Discover the history of your town's cemetery with etchings of gravestones.

Gather
- Tracing paper
- Charcoal or sidewalk chalk
- Regular paper
- Manila folder

Go
1. Call your local library and find out where the public cemeteries near your house are. Try to find one at least 110 years old.
2. Go to the cemetery and look at the gravestones. Choose one or two interesting ones.
3. Help your child lay his tracing paper on the tombstone. Let him gently rub the paper with charcoal or sidewalk chalk.
4. To keep the etchings clean, put them between sheets of clean paper and slip them inside a manila folder.
5. Take them home and discuss what the symbols might mean.

Grow
Christians can look forward to spending eternity in paradise. While you are taking a look at old cemeteries with your child, you can help him gain a new perspective on death. Yes, separation from a loved one is sad. But if the person knew Jesus as his Savior and your child does too, then someday they'll be together again in a place that's better than he can imagine.

ꙮ ꙮ ꙮ

16

Sky Lights

Ages 6 and up
by Shellie Hurrle

Use these questions and answers to discuss lightning storms with your children.

What is lightning?
To put it simply, lightning is electricity. It's made of electrons, which are negatively

charged electrical particles. Electricity is usually invisible, but the extremely high voltage of a lightning bolt—up to one hundred million volts—causes the air it passes through to glow. Thunderstorms and lightning occurs most often during hot summer afternoons and evenings. However, lightning can happen at any time—even during a snowstorm.

How big are lightning bolts, and how long does the flash last?
Lightning can be 10 miles long, but on the average, it's approximately 4 miles long and about 1 inch wide. Lightning travels up to 60,000 miles per second. Flashes of lightning last only 1/10,000 of a second. Humans see it longer because a picture of it forms in our eyes, allowing us to see it even after it fades away.

How can I avoid being struck by lightning?
The safest place to be during a thunderstorm is in the house. Always stay away from electrical appliances, especially the television. Don't go near metal objects. Water is a good conductor of electricity, so save your shower until after the storm. If you get caught outside in a thunderstorm, try to get inside a car and close the windows. This may sound strange because metal attracts lightning, but the grounded steel of the car passes the current safely into the ground.

What should I do if I'm outside and can't get to shelter?
Be sure to stay away from water. Move away from ponds, pools, and lakes. Stay near the ground because lightning strikes taller objects, but don't ever lie flat. Instead, crouch down with your hands around your knees. If you're with a group of people in an open space, spread out. If you're in the forest, try not to stand near tall trees. Find a group of low trees growing close together.

Is there anything good about lightning?
Lightning definitely has its benefits. It cleans the air by leaving behind ozone (a special type of oxygen). We need ozone to screen out harmful rays from the sun. Lightning also balances the natural electricity between the earth and sky. Perhaps most importantly, the rain that falls with lightning is rich in nitrogen—an important gas for all living things.

Why does it thunder after lightning flashes?
The temperature of lightning bolts can be thousands of degrees (even hotter than the sun); therefore, they heat up the air. Explosive expansion and contraction of air cause pressure pulses that are heard as rumbles and crashes. The flash and the sound occur at the same time, but because light travels faster than sound, we see lightning before we hear thunder.

Can you measure how far away the lightning struck?
When you first see a flash of lightning, count the seconds until you hear the thunder. Every 5 seconds counted means the lightning is one mile away. For example, if it takes 10 seconds to hear the thunder, the lightning is two miles away. If you don't hear thunder, the storm is probably very far away. If the lightning and thunder happen almost simultaneously (within 5 seconds or less), you'd better watch out. The lightning is close. Lightning kills nearly 100 people in the United States and injures more than 200 each year.

What's most damaging about lightning?
Lightning is dangerous not only to humans but to forest creatures and vegetation. It's the leading cause of forest fires. In the Rocky Mountains, lightning causes more than 9,000 fires every year.

How often does lightning strike?
Lightning is more common than most people realize. More than 100,000 thunderstorms occur every hour around the world. Every second, nearly 100 lightning bolts strike the earth. An old expression says lightning never strikes the same place twice, but this is a myth. It fact, lightning can strike the same place repeatedly during a single thunderstorm.

Grow

Do lightning bolts give your kids the jolts? If your child is afraid of lightning storms, learn Psalm 56:3 together: "When I am afraid, I will trust in you. In God, whose word I praise, in God I trust; I will not be afraid."

17

Star Search

Use these "star-tling" facts to learn more about God's heavens.

Constellation Clues

Ages 8 and up

Gather
- Clear night with no moon or a small moon
- Old blanket
- Flashlight
- Red nail polish

Go
1. Wait for a clear night when the moon is small or—better yet—not visible. Then grab an old blanket and head outside.
2. Bring a flashlight, too, so your child can follow the directions in this book. But cover the flashlight lens with red nail polish so your child's eyes can adjust to the dark.

3. Have your child lie down on her back so her head is toward the north and her feet toward the south. Then try to find some of the stars and constellations on the previous page. A star chart from the library may be helpful, too.

4. Summer is the best time to see the Milky Way, that white band across the night sky made of billions of stars. What you see is the heart of our own galaxy. The stars we see from Earth have been grouped into 88 different pictures (such as a Big Dipper). Only about 24 constellations can be seen in the sky at the same time. Let your child try to find these three:

- **Cygnus** (sig-nus) looks like a swan. Part of this large constellation is known as the Northern Cross. Deneb, a bright star, marks the tail of the swan, and together with Vega and Altair makes up the "Summer Triangle."
- **Lyra** (lye-ra)—meaning a harp-like musical instrument—includes the brilliant bluish star called Vega. It is the fifth brightest star in the sky and in 1850 was the first star ever to have its photograph taken.
- **Aquila** (ack-will-a) is a picture of an enormous eagle. At its head is a very bright star called Altair.

Surprising Star Stats
Ages 8 and up

Give your child this quiz to find out her "star" potential.

How many stars are in our galaxy?
Our galaxy has about one hundred billion stars, but even under ideal conditions, only two thousand of them are visible without a telescope.

Why do stars blink?
Stars appear to twinkle because you are looking through Earth's atmosphere to see them. It's like looking up at a streetlight from the bottom of a swimming pool.

Why does the sun look yellow, but other stars white?
If you look closely, you'll see that not all stars are silvery white. The hottest stars are blue; then comes green, white, yellow, and orange. Red stars play it "cool"—only 4,900° Fahrenheit!

What is a shooting star?
"Shooting stars" aren't stars at all. They are little pieces of rock that burn up when they enter the earth's atmosphere. August is one of the best months to see these "meteors," especially around the constellation called Perseus. By the way, if you see a "meteor" that's moving very slowly, it's probably just a satellite.

Grow
Choose one or two of these stellar Bible verses to memorize this summer. If your child needs help with fun ways to memorize Scripture, see "Word Games" on page 43.

- "God made two great lights—the greater light to govern the day and the lesser light to govern the night. He also made the stars. . . . And God saw that it was good." (Genesis 1:16, 18b)
- "The heavens declare the glory of God; the skies proclaim the work of his hands. Day after day they pour forth speech; night after night they display knowledge." (Psalm 19:1-2)
- "He determines the number of the stars and calls them each by name." (Psalm 147:4)
- "He who made the Pleiades and Orion . . . the LORD is his name." (Amos 5:8)

ℰ ℰ ℰ

18

Weather Watch

Build your own meteorology equipment.

Water Gauge

Ages 7 and up

Measure the rain summer storms yield.

Gather
- Plastic, 1-liter soda bottle
- Scissors or knife
- Vinyl or other waterproof tape
- Clean pebbles or marbles

Go
Your child should be able to help with most of these steps.
1. Remove the label from the bottle and clean the bottle thoroughly.
2. Cut off the top of the bottle about five inches down from the neck.
3. Using vinyl tape, cover the cut edges of both parts of the bottle.
4. Stick a strip of tape on the outside of the bottle, two inches from the bottom.
5. Put six small pieces of tape $1/2$ inch from each other, going up the bottle, beginning with the bottom strip of tape.
6. Drop some clean pebbles or marbles into the bottle for weight.
7. Pour in enough water to reach the bottom tape mark.
8. Wedge the top half of the bottle, neck down, into the bottom half.

9. Tape the funnel in place and set the gauge in a level, open spot outdoors away from buildings or trees.
10. Wait for rain.
11. Besides measuring rain, your child can also use the gauge to measure how much water your sprinklers put out. Set the gauge in the center of your lawn and turn on the sprinklers. After 10 minutes, read the gauge. With this information, your child is ready to help decide how much to water the lawn by checking the recorded rainfall levels in the newspaper.
12. After each measurement, empty the gauge, leaving just enough water to reach the bottom of the tape.

Pressure Looker

Ages 7 and up

Meteorologists use barometers to determine air pressure. When air pressure is high, the weather is likely to be clear; when air pressure is low, a storm may be coming. To find out if you're in for some rain, make a barometer for your backyard.

Gather
- Water
- Paper
- Tape
- Food coloring
- Narrow-necked bottle (like a ketchup bottle)
- Shallow bowl with a flat bottom

Go

Your child should be able to help with most of the steps.
1. Clean the bottle completely.
2. Add some food coloring and fill the bottle to the brim with water.
3. Fill the bowl with about two inches of water. Add a few drops of food coloring.
4. Holding your fingers over the opening, tip the bottle over and place it upside down in the bowl.
5. Draw lines every $1/8$ inch on a 5-inch strip of paper. Tape the paper to the bottle so the middle of the strip is at the level of the water.
6. Encourage your child to watch the barometer from day to day and keep a record. When the air pressure rises, it will push harder on the water in the bowl, moving some of it up into the bottle. When the pressure drops, more of the water will drain into the bowl.

Where the Wind Blows

Ages 7 and up

East, South, West, or North—From where does the wind come forth?

Gather

- 10-inch piece of heavy wire (like from a coat hanger)
- Piece of thin cardboard (like a manila file folder)
- Permanent marker
- Scissors
- Tape
- 3 plastic straws
- Ballpoint pen cap
- Stapler

Go

Your child should be able to help with most of these steps.

1. Cut out an arrow's head and tail from the cardboard. Staple them to the ends of a straw.
2. Tape the center of the straw to the top of the pen cap.
3. Cut the other two straws in half.
4. Cut four circles from the cardboard. Mark them N, E, S, and W for north, east, south, and west.
5. Staple each circle to the end of a straw piece.
6. Tape the straw pieces to the wire about 5 inches from the end. They should be at right angles to each other.
7. Put one end of the wire into the pen cap.
8. Hold the wind vane in your hand, or attach it to a post. Be sure to point the N toward the north. When there's some wind, the arrow will point in the direction it's blowing.

Grow

"He causes his sun to rise on the evil and the good, and sends rain on the righteous and the unrighteous" (Matthew 5:45). God gives us everything we need to live (like rain to grow food). What are some of the good things God has "showered" on your family this summer?

SECTION SEVEN

Indoor Activities

19

Air Hockey

Ages 7 and up

Blow off an afternoon with this fast-paced game.

Gather
- Table
- Goalposts (salt and pepper shakers, water glasses, etc.)
- Ping-Pong ball
- One or two kids

Go
1. Set up the goalposts on both ends of the table.
2. Place a Ping-Pong ball in the middle of the table and say "Start."
3. Each player blows until she has huffed and puffed the ball through her opponent's goal.
4. If only one child is playing, she can see how few puffs it takes to get the ball through the goal.

Grow
Stage a tournament for some of the kids in your neighborhood. This is a game where athletic prowess takes a backseat and anyone can "compete."

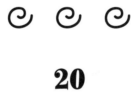

20

Copy Cat

Ages 7 and up

Here's how to trace any picture using a table lamp and a piece of glass.

Gather
- A picture from a magazine or a photograph
- White paper
- Glass from a picture frame
- Lamp
- Pencil

Go

1. Place the picture on the table and the white paper to the right of it.
2. Hold the glass up and down between the picture and the paper.
3. Turn on the lamp so it's shining above and to the left of the picture.
4. Look through the glass from the left to the blank page. The picture's image is reflected there. Let your child trace over the image on the white paper.

Grow

As your child copies the image on the paper, discuss some New Testament passages that encourage us to imitate Christ's example (1 Corinthians 11:1, Ephesians 5:1). Ask your child to think of ways he can "look" more like Jesus.

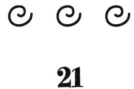

21

Fingerprint Finders

Ages 8 and up

Do your kids want to be detectives? Start their training now.

Gather
- Baby powder
- Transparent tape
- Large, soft paintbrush, or a makeup powder brush
- Facial tissues
- Magnifying glass
- Black or other dark-colored construction paper

Go

1. To begin, let your child sprinkle some baby powder over the place he has chosen to look for fingerprints. Try doorknobs, windows, coffee tables, countertops, magazines, the car, or water glasses. Or do you just want to know who opened the cookie jar? You may have to wipe these areas clean first to prevent grime and buildup from marring the print.
2. Very lightly, he should brush the powder on the surface until it is a fine dust. If he has been gentle enough, fingerprints should appear.
3. To pick up the print, let him carefully put a piece of tape over it.
4. Then he should lift the tape quickly and stick it on a piece of dark paper.
5. To look closer, use the magnifying glass.
6. Help him make a chart of everyone's fingerprints in your family to see whose fingerprint is whose. Does everyone's fingerprint swirl or tilt the same way? How can you tell if it is a right-handed or left-handed fingerprint?

Grow

Have your kids think about how many different fingerprints there are in the world. God has made each one of us unique and special. How He loves us!

॰ ॰ ॰

22

Ice Fishing

Ages 4 and up

Catch on to this experiment using a piece of string and an ice cube.

Gather
- Piece of thread about 8 inches long
- One straw
- Ice cube
- Glass of cold water
- Salt

Go
1. Let your child tie one end of the string to the end of the straw. Dip the string in water.
2. Place the ice cube in the glass of water, making sure it gets wet.
3. Let the ice cube float on the water. Ask your child to lay the loose end of the string across the top of the ice cube.
4. She can then sprinkle a pinch or two of salt on the string.
5. Count slowly to 30, and then ask her to gently lift the string. The string should be sticking to the cube with enough adhesion to lift the ice cube out of the water.

Grow

This experiment works because the salt first makes the water on top of the ice cube very cold, and then the salt dissolves in the rest of the water. The water on top of the ice cube freezes, allowing the string to stick. In Matthew 5:13, Jesus said, "You are the salt of the earth." Talk to your kids about the difference they can make as "salt" in the lives of their friends and family.

23

Paper Power

Ages 6 and up

This brain teaser will "stretch" paper—and your child's perspective.

Gather
- 8¹/₂-by-11-inch piece of paper
- Scissors
- Ruler
- Pencil

Go

1. Show your child the sheet of paper. Ask her, "Will this paper wrap all the way around you?" She should shake her head no.
2. Trim 2¹/₂ inches from one end of the paper so that you have an 8¹/₂-inch square.
3. Fold it in half.
4. Make five marks along the fold that are an equal distance apart. That's just over 1¹/₄ inches between marks.
5. At every mark cut 3 inches of the way to the other side.
6. Cut along the fold from the first cut to the last cut.
7. Make four marks along the open edge, one in between each slice.
8. Cut at every mark 3 inches of the way to the side with the fold.
9. Unfold the square, pull open the ring, and put it over your child's head.

Grow

God often makes use of the "paper trick." We don't think what we have is enough, but it manages to stretch and fulfill our needs. Have you ever thought you were in want, but in reality really had everything you needed? Tell your child about what God has done for you.

⊙ ⊙ ⊙

24

Shadow Animals

Ages 4 and up

Put the spotlight on your child's imagination by making these finger friends come alive.

Gather
- Dark room
- Flashlight or desk lamp

Go
1. Turn off the lights and draw the blinds. Shine a light against an empty wall or door.
2. Show your child how to make these animal shapes: ostrich, horse, butterfly, crab.
3. Make up a play and use the shadows as the characters.

Grow
Have your kids use Bible stories that include animals for their shadow play; for example, Daniel in the lions' den (Daniel 6), Balaam's donkey (Numbers 22:21-31).

25

Rainbow in a Bowl

Ages 4 and up

With a mirror, water, and paper, your child can create a bright arc of color.

Gather
- Mirror
- Bowl of water
- Flashlight
- White paper

Go
1. Place the mirror in the bowl of water, so it's leaning against the side.
2. Let your child shine the flashlight at the part of the mirror that's under water.
3. Hold the paper above the mirror. Position the paper until you see a rainbow on the page.
4. Ask your child to experiment shining the flashlight in different positions to see which reveals the best colors.

Grow
Now that you can see a rainbow any time you want to, don't forget what they really signify. Read Genesis 9:8-17 aloud to remind your child about God's faithfulness.

26

Seven-Layer Suit-Up

Ages 4 and up

Heat up some action with this "clothes-circuit" relay game.

Gather
- Two outfits of winter clothes: jacket, hat, gloves, scarf, socks, boots, and pants. (Hint: Adult clothes work the best. Make sure all the clothes will fit the largest child who is playing.)
- Bunch of kids
- Two bags large enough to hold all the clothes

Go
1. Pack each bag with one winter outfit.
2. Divide the children into two teams. The first person on each team gets a bag of clothes.
3. When the race starts, unpack your bag and put on the outfit over your summer clothes.
4. Run to the end of the room and back.
5. Take off the winter wardrobe and pack the bag for the next person to go.
6. The first team that finishes bundling, running, and bagging wins.

Grow

The New Testament teaches to give even if it puts the giver in want (Luke 6:29). Now that you have all the winter clothes out, sort through them, and donate your extra "tunics" to a homeless shelter. With your children, discuss what "extra" things you can give away so that others might be warm in the coming winter.

27

Stunts that Stump

Try these tricks to amaze and entertain friends!

Rubbing It In

Ages 8 and up

Make a coin disappear.

Gather
- Coin
- Short-sleeved shirt

Go

These instructions are for kids to read to themselves.
1. Wearing short sleeves, rest one elbow on the table with your hand at your neck. Hold a coin in the palm of your other hand. Now tell your audience you are going to rub the coin against your arm until it disappears. Begin rubbing it up and down your arm.
2. Accidentally-on-purpose let the coin slip and fall on the table. Pick up the coin with the non-rubbing hand and pass it to your rubbing hand. Repeat the steps, again letting it accidentally-on-purpose fall to the table. Looking frustrated, pick it up as before and begin rubbing.

3. When you "accidentally" let it fall a third time, pick it up (as before) with your non-rubbing hand, but only pretend to pass it to your rubbing hand.
4. Begin rubbing again as if the coin was there, while secretly dropping it down your shirt with the other hand. Then—presto!—show them it's gone.

Three's the Charm

Ages 8 and up

A coin disappears—then one, two, three, it's back again.

Gather
 • 3 coins, all alike

Go
These instructions are for kids to read to themselves.
1. Hold two coins between your thumb and forefinger. Secretly conceal a third coin in your palm underneath your ring and pinkie fingers.
2. Tell your audience you will make another coin appear by rubbing them together. Quickly rub the coins back and forth. It will look as though you have three coins.
3. Once your audience has seen the optical illusion, drop the coins, including the one you had hidden in your palm, on the table.

Where Did It Go?

Ages 8 and up

A piece of paper seems to swallow a coin.

Gather
 • 2 identical pieces of construction paper
 • Coin

Go
1. Before you perform this trick, fold two identical pieces of colored paper into thirds and into thirds again. Unfolded, each piece should be divided into nine equal squares. Refold the pieces of paper and stick the backs together with tape. Unfold one piece and lay it out on the table with the folded piece hidden beneath.
2. When you're ready to do the trick, place a coin in the center square of the unfolded sheet. Fold the paper around it. Then pick up the packet and flash it quickly before the audience, turning it over without them realizing it.
3. Lay the paper down on the table and unfold it. The coin is gone.
4. To make the coin "reappear," fold the paper back up. Turn the packet over and unfold it.

Chalk Walk

Ages 8 and up

Show how chalk can appear to pass through a table.

Gather
- White chalk

Go
1. When no one is looking, rub a heavy amount of chalk on the fingernail of your middle finger. Now open your hand and show people that there's no chalk mark on your palm.
2. Ask someone to pick a spot on the table and draw a mark there. Then announce that you are going to rub the chalk mark through the table onto your palm.
3. Reach your palm under the table so it's beneath the chalk spot. Rub out the chalk mark on the table with one hand. Meanwhile, curl up the fingers of your hidden hand so the chalk on your fingernail touches your palm. (No one will see you do this.)
4. Open your hand and bring it out from under the table. People will be amazed to see the chalk mark on your palm!

Dot-to-Dot

Ages 8 and up

An optical illusion that makes spots vanish into thin air.

Gather
- Craft stick

Go

These instructions are for kids to read to themselves.
1. Sand or whittle down one end of a craft stick until it is nearly round and rolls easily between your thumb and first finger. On one side of the flat end, draw one large dot.
2. Hold the small end of the craft stick and practice flipping it over with your wrist, as shown. Now try it again, at the same time twisting the craft stick between your thumb and finger so the other side is facing up. (It happens so fast, no one can see that you're twisting it.)
3. With a little practice, you can make it look like there's a dot on both sides, or like the dot is traveling from side to side, or like all dots have disappeared! (You can also try this with a flat toothpick.)

Grow

Some people may be tempted to call these tricks "magic," but they are only optical illusions or sleight-of-hand deceptions. While it is fun to fool people with a party trick or game like those above, it is wrong to lie, deceive, or to cover up wrongdoing, especially if it is planned and rehearsed. Remind your child that the Lord honors honesty, as is shown in Psalm 24:3-4, "Who may ascend the hill of the LORD? Who may stand in his holy place? He who has clean hands and a pure heart."

ᴄ ᴄ ᴄ

28

Inside Scoop

Still stuck for ideas? Here are eight simple ways to have more indoor fun.

Go
1. **Start a collection.** Try something easy to find, such as bottle caps, bookmarks, or buttons. Let your child decide how to organize and display them. Egg cartons and shoe boxes make great display cases.
2. **Open a children's dictionary and pick a funny word.** Ask your child to give a definition—or make up his own. Let him pick the next word and guess the meaning.
3. **Plan a meal in which all the food names start with the same letter or all the food is the same color.** Try S: spaghetti, salad, sourdough bread, strawberries, and soda. Orange works well in summer: cantaloupe, macaroni and cheese, carrots, and orange juice.
4. **Paint faces.** Keep face paints (special paints found at the craft store) on hand to decorate a smile. If you're brave, let your child paint your face.
5. **Freeze gummy worms in paper cups filled with lemonade or white grape juice.** Cover the cups with foil and insert craft sticks.
6. **Decorate a small notebook with stickers, markers, and glitter.** Write a funny or nice message to your child and hide the notebook in her room. When she finds it, let her write a message back to you and hide it in your room. Keep hiding the notebook until all the pages are full. Then start again.
7. **Decorate pieces of cardboard and turn them into a message holder.** Use scraps of lace, material, and ribbon to decorate a small piece of cardboard. Print a happy message on it with puff paint. Glue a clothespin on the back. Let dry. Then glue a piece of magnetic strip to the clothespin. Hang it on the refrigerator and use it to post cheerful messages.—*Lauren Canitia*
8. **Make edible clay.** Combine 2 cups powdered milk, 2 cups peanut butter, and 1 cup honey. Mix well. Give it to your kids so they can shape and pound.—*Brandon Cloud*

SECTION EIGHT

Outdoor Activities

29

Backyard Safari

Ages 6 and up

Your children will discover a new appreciation for the outdoors on this delightful "field trip."

Gather
- Paper
- Graph paper
- Pencil
- Your backyard, a park, or the wide-open outdoors

Go
1. Make a list of things your child can find in the yard or park such as flowers, berries, pinecones, feathers, seeds, rocks, dandelions, sow bugs, one-pointed leaves, and five-pointed leaves.
2. If your child can't read, draw a picture of each item.
3. Give him the list so he can collect the items on his own, or join him in the search.
4. Give an older child a piece of graph paper. Make a map by marking three or four landmarks on the grid so your child has reference points.
5. Have him mark the paper where he finds the listed items.
6. Put the items in his "Nature Notebook." (See page 78 for instructions.)

Grow
When everything has been collected, look in Genesis 1 to find out on which day these items were created.

30

Bubble Bonanza

Ages 4 and up

Kids will bubble over with enthusiasm while making and using their own soap mixture and bubble-blowing utensils.

Gather
- Clean pail
- 10 cups water
- 1 cup liquid dish soap (Dawn brand seems to produce the sturdiest bubbles.)

- 4 tablespoons glycerin or white corn syrup (Glycerin is a syrupy liquid that you can buy at a drugstore. It helps the bubbles get bigger and last longer.)
- Stiff wire
- Heavy string
- Funnel (optional)
- Straws taped together (optional)
- Paper towel tube (optional)
- Can opened on both sides (optional)
- Plastic rings from a soda six-pack (optional)

Go

1. Pour the 10 cups of water into the pail. Add the cup of dish washing soap and 4 table-spoons glycerin.
2. Mix well, but don't stir too fast. (Suds make it harder to blow bubbles.)
3. Scoop any froth off the top. Let the mixture sit for a few minutes.
4. While older children can make their own wands, younger children will need assistance. Bend the wire into a loop at least 4 inches in diameter. Leave enough wire to form a handle.
5. String will help the bubble solution stick to the wand. Wrap the string spirally around the loop.
6. To give the handle a good "grip," wrap it tightly with string.
7. Let your children dip their wands in and out of the liquid until a film appears over the opening. Huff and puff away.
8. When they get the hang of the wand, let them experiment with the different bubble blowers listed above.
9. Ask your children what happens when they blow hard through the loop. Blow softly through the loop. Jerk the loop through the air. Wave the loop smoothly. Catch the bubble with dry hands. Catch the bubble with soapy hands.

Bubble Olympics

Set up a contest to see who can win these six silly games.

1. Bouncing Bubbles: Whose bubble goes the farthest? Blow from the same place, follow your bubble and stand where it pops.
2. Abundant Bubbles: Who can blow the most bubbles with one breath?
3. Double Bubbles: Who can blow two bubbles stuck together? Who can blow the most double bubbles?
4. Bag a Bubble: Who can hold a bubble the longest? Catch a bubble with soapy hands and then be very still until it pops.
5. Bubble Bull's-Eye: Who can come closest to hitting a target by moving a bubble with his breath?
6. Big Bubbles: Who can blow the largest single bubble?

Grow

Do your older children baby-sit? Bubbles are great fun for kids of all ages. Suggest they bring their bubble supplies with them the next time they have a job. They'll have a good time or bust!

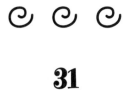

31

Bug Abodes

Keep some creepy crawlies at home for close inspection.

Caterpillar Cottage

Ages 4 and up

Gather
- Large jar
- Newspaper
- Nylon stocking
- Rubber band

Go
1. Turn a large jar on its side.
2. Let your child place several small sheets of newspaper in the "bottom."
3. Help him cover the jar's mouth with a piece of nylon stocking and wrap a rubber band around it.
4. When your child finds a caterpillar, make sure he collects some of the leaves it was eating. (Monarch caterpillars eat milkweed. Cabbage butterfly caterpillars eat cabbage and nasturtiums.)
5. The caterpillar will need a fresh supply of leaves every day. Just have your child slide out the old newspapers and put in some new paper and leaves every day.
6. Soon the caterpillar will spin a cocoon. When the butterfly (or you may have a moth instead) comes out, let it go after its wings are dry.

Ladybug Palace

Ages 4 and up

Gather
- Jar and lid with holes poked in it
- Cardboard
- Clear plastic cup about $3^1/_2$ inches wide

Go

1. Let your child catch four or five ladybugs and put them in the jar.
2. Put the jar in the refrigerator for about an hour to slow the ladybugs down.
3. Slide the ladybugs out of the jar and onto the cardboard.
4. Put the cup on top of them.
5. Feed them leaves with tiny aphids (green, white, brown, or gray insects) on them.
6. Keep the ladybugs for a day or so and then set them free.

Beetle Barracks

Ages 4 and up

Gather
- 8-ounce yogurt container or medium-sized tin can
- Apple core or hard-boiled egg
- Milk carton
- Nylon stocking

Go

1. Let your child dig a shallow hole in the yard and fit an 8-ounce yogurt cup or tin can inside.
2. Drop an apple core or hard-boiled egg inside.
3. Help him partially cover the trap with a flat rock raised on small stones to give the bugs shade once they fall in.
4. Your child should check the trap every morning. If no beetles come in a day or so, try a different spot.
5. To keep the bugs, you'll need a milk-carton cage. Wash and dry the carton. Cut 2- by 5-inch windows in the side.
6. Ask your child to put some food, grass, sticks, rocks, and leaves in the bottom. He can slip a sheer nylon stocking over the entire carton.
7. Let him keep the beetles overnight and let them creep away.

Cricket Cage

Ages 4 and up

Gather
- Large glass jar
- Nylon stocking
- Rubber band
- Sand
- Twigs
- Leaves
- Cotton balls

Go

1. Let your child put sand, twigs, and leaves in the bottom of the jar.
2. After he catches a cricket and puts it in the jar, help him cover the top with the nylon stocking and secure it with a rubber band.
3. Crickets will eat cut-up potatoes, bits of meat, melons, or almost any fruit or vegetables. Give the cricket fresh food every day.
4. Here are some tips for making the cricket comfortable: Keep the sand damp. Crickets don't like sun; they prefer shade. Keep a piece of moist cotton in the jar so the cricket will have enough water.
5. Only male crickets chirp. If you get one that makes too much noise at night, put it back outside and find a quieter cricket.

Grow

Did you know that God allowed the Israelites to eat four kinds of winged insects? Leviticus 11:21-22 says the katydid, cricket, locust, and grasshopper are okay to munch on. (Pass the ketchup, yum, yum!) All of those bugs have jointed legs. Next time your child catches one, examine it with a magnifying glass and check out the knobby knees.

℮ ℮ ℮

32

Fine Feathered Fun

by Katherine G. Bond

"Look at the birds of the air…your heavenly Father feeds them" (Matthew 6:26). Teach your children how to appreciate God's plan for the birds with these "birds-on-the-brain" ideas.

Bird Bait

Ages 4 and up

Here's how you can lure birds to come close to your home. There's no better invitation than nuts and popcorn.

Gather
- Popcorn
- Peanuts
- Stale bread
- Breakfast cereal (low sugar and salt)
- Large plastic embroidery needle
- Thread

Go

1. Let your children make a string of peanuts in their shells, using a plastic embroidery needle and thread. You can also string popcorn or squares of stale bread.
2. Hang the garland between trees or drape it on one. Then watch your party guests nibble and peck.

Sneak Up on a Swallow

Ages 6 and up

Let your children try these tricks to get a closer look at their flying friends.

Gather
- Library book about birds in your area
- Pad of paper
- Pencil
- Clothes that blend with plants and trees

Go

1. Moving slowly, let your child go into a nature area or backyard wearing clothes the same colors as the plants and trees.
2. Help her find a hiding spot.
3. Show her how to make a kissing sound on the back of her hand. Curious birds may come closer.
4. Ask her to take notes on what the birds eat, where they drink, or where their nests are.
5. Be sure she listens to their noises. What does each one sound like?
6. If she spots a new bird, let her watch it until it moves away. Encourage her to remember what she saw and jot down notes. What color was it? Was it big or small? Did it have special stripes or spots? What was the shape of its beak?
7. Try to identify the new bird by finding it in the library book.

Grow

If your kids want to attract birds and feed them on a regular basis, make a bird feeder like "For the Birds" on page 148. There are several birds mentioned in Scripture. Brainstorm with your child and see how many you can think of. Then check out these references for birds in the Bible (Some are familiar and some are obscure!): Genesis 1:20, 8:6-12; Leviticus 11:13-19; 1 Kings 17:1-6; Proverbs 30:29-31; Matthew 8:20, 10:29-31, 21:12, 23:37; Mark 4:4; Luke 3:22, 12:24, 22:34, 54-62.

33

Hares and Hounds

Ages 4 and up

Like Hansel and Gretel, your children will love making and following a trail of bread crumbs and pebbles.

Gather
- 2 or more players
- Park or large backyard
- 10 bread pieces and 10 pebbles each marked with the numbers 1 through 10
- Bag (for bread and pebbles)

Go
1. Choose one person or team of kids to be the hare(s). If the children playing are very young, you will want to help with this job.
2. The other person or team is the hound(s).
3. The hare hides the pebbles in order around the yard or park. He drops the corresponding bread piece near the hidden pebbles as clues. For example, if a pebble is hidden in a tree knot, the bread piece would be dropped near the tree.
4. The hound follows the trail of bread pieces and collects the pebbles.
5. To make the game more difficult for older children, give the hounds a time limit.
6. When all the pebbles are found, the hare and hound switch places.
7. After you are done with the game, leave the bread pieces for the birds.

Grow
Spend some fun time with your child by treating him to an after-dark game. Plan a game night when adult friends or family are visiting. After sunset, give the teams flashlights and begin the hunt. Be sure to laugh together lots!

34

Mirror Messages

Ages 7 and up

Long ago people used the sun to send messages over distances as great as 50 miles. Here's how your family can use the sun to send "flash mail."

Gather
- Hand mirror
- 2 players
- Pad of paper (optional)
- Pencil (optional)

Go

1. On a sunny day, let one child stand in your front yard and hold the mirror so the sun is shining into it. Be sure to warn him not to shine it directly into someone's eyes.
2. The other child should be down the street a ways, but within shouting distance until they get the hang of the system.
3. Help the child holding the mirror tilt it until the other child can see a flash of light.
4. Let the children develop a simple code. For example two quick flashes could mean "yes."
5. Older children can see how far away they can send "flash mail." Or they can experiment with International Morse Code. The asterisks represent short flashes, the dashes long flashes. A short pause is expected between letters, a longer pause between words. They will need a pad of paper and a pencil to write down the code for translation.

A = * –	B = –* * *	C = –* – *	D = – * *	E = *
F = * *–*	G = – – *	H = * * * *	I = * *	J = *– – –
K = –*–	L =*–**	M =– –	N =–*	O =– – –
P =* – –*	Q =– – *	R =*–*	S =***	T =–
U =**–	V =***–	W =*– –	X =–**–	Y =–*– –
Z =– –**				

Grow

Ask your children about the ways that God communicates with us. Share a time that you or your child believed God was speaking to you.

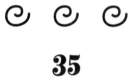

35

Nature Photography

Ages 7 and up

By introducing your child to photography, you may help him or her develop a lifelong hobby or even a career.

Gather
- Camera
- Film
- Clear day

Go

The following tips will help your child take good photographs.

1. If possible, choose a background that isn't too busy.
2. If what you are looking at isn't interesting, sit down on the ground or a rock and look up. Or stand on something steady and look down.
3. Try to have the sun at your back, but watch for your shadow in the picture you are going to take.
4. Cloudy days can also be great for picture taking.
5. Keep the horizon straight in your viewfinder and hold the camera steady. Be sure your finger isn't in front of the lens.
6. Don't hesitate to get close to the person or object you are going to photograph.
7. Instead of backing up for tall objects or people, turn the camera on its side.
8. Many wildflowers blossom and die quickly. They will live forever in a photo.
9. Keep your eyes open for wildlife, big and small.
10. Wild berries make colorful pictures. Look for them on bushes.
11. Butterflies are easier to photograph in the morning because they move more slowly in the cooler temperatures.

Grow

Keep the camera ready for candid shots inside and outside. Enlarge and frame your child's best photos. Communicate your love to your child by showing off his or her photos. And remind your child that he or she is special to God as well.

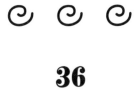

36

Summertime Scrapbook

Ages 7 and up

By keeping a nature journal, your child will learn about God's creation and wonder at His handiwork.

Gather
- Spiral notebook or "Nature Notebook" (directions below)
- Bible

Go

Choose which activities listed below are best for your children. Record their findings in the Nature Notebook or a spiral notebook. After they catch on to the process, let them come up with their own ideas.

1. Use the following Bible verses about nature as conversation starters about God's majesty: Psalm 1:1-3 and Isaiah 40:6-8, 55:10-13. Keep these verses in mind when working with your child's Nature Notebook. Older children will want to copy the Scriptures into their notebooks.
2. Record the weather for a week. Take morning and evening temperature readings or get them from the newspaper. Have her draw pictures of clouds and the position of the sun in the sky.
3. Make a water gauge (instructions on page 51) and record the amount of rain that falls in your backyard.
4. Ask your child to draw pictures of real bugs he has seen. Then ask him to draw an imaginary bug.
5. Take photographs of your child in the park or wilderness or help him take pictures himself. (See the photography tips on page 77.)
6. Encourage your child to write about what she sees, smells, hears, and feels in the yard at different times of the day.
7. Write down a story that your child makes up about the park and the creatures he found there.
8. Glue in leaves, pressed flowers, and colorful rubbings of tree bark, leaves, or rocks.

Nature Notebook

Ages 6 and up

Create a nature scrapbook to record special outdoor memories.

Gather
- 4 or 5 sheets of plain paper
- Sheet of construction paper
- Scissors
- Hole punch
- Stapler
- 12 inches of yarn
- Pencil

Go
Help your children create this simple book.
1. Fold the plain paper in half and cut it along the crease.
2. Stack the papers together and fold the construction paper around it so the crease in the construction paper is on the cut edge of the plain paper.
3. Staple the pages together along the left margin.
4. Punch a hole near the folded edge and tie on a pencil with the piece of yarn.
5. Let your children decorate the cover with drawings, pebbles, nature impressions, or pressed plants.

Grow

Proverbs 3:19 says, "By wisdom the LORD laid the earth's foundations, by understanding he set the heavens in place." What evidence can your child find that proves the world was made by an intelligent Creator?

37

Sunflower Fun

Ages 4 and up

Watch your kids' faces bloom when they harvest their own sunflowers.

Gather
- Raw sunflower seeds
- Sunny spot in your backyard
- Spade
- Garden stakes (optional)

Go
1. As soon as the threat of frost is gone, dig a hole 2 inches deep for each sunflower seed. Make the holes 4 inches apart. It's easiest if they grow near a fence so you can tie them to the posts. Otherwise you'll need to use tall stakes as support.
2. Let your child drop the seed in and cover it with dirt.
3. Help your child water the seeds every day.
4. Wait 7 to 10 days for a sprout, and 8 to 12 weeks for the whole thing to bloom.
5. When the flowers grow about four feet tall, tie them to the fence or a stake.
6. At the end of the summer, the flowers will die. Take the seeds out and feed them to the birds.
7. Or roast them at 250° for 45 minutes, and let your family crunch away.
8. Be sure to keep a handful of uncooked seeds to plant next year.

Grow

Have you ever noticed that plants grow toward the sun? As you watch the sunflowers sprout and grow, they will serve as a reminder for your children to grow in the direction of the "Son."

ℰ   ℰ   ℰ

38

Sandcastles in the Sun

Ages 4 and up

Grab a pail and a shovel and head for the beach.

Gather
- Spade or large shovel
- Small shovel
- Plastic bucket
- Plastic cups, assorted sizes
- Ruler
- Camera (optional)

Go
1. If you are going to the beach, be sure to build your castle one or two hours after high tide. Pick a good, hard, level spot for the foundation of your child's castle. Keep away from coarse or pebbly sand and stones and seashells. These will weaken the castle once it dries.
2. Let your child pile up a large mound of damp sand. Help him sift out stones, shells, and crabs if any. Pack the mound and level the top.
3. Show your child how to scoop handfuls of sand into the pail, packing down each handful. Pack the last scoopful of sand well and level off the top.
4. Let him carefully turn his pail upside down on top of the mound. Thump gently on the pail's bottom. Remove the pail and reveal a sand tower. If it crumbles, experiment with more or less water and try again.
5. Together, build a second tower just like the first. Place it about 3 inches from the first.
6. With damp sand, help your child fill in the space between the towers, packing the sides tightly.
7. Let him fill up a small plastic cup as he did the pail. Turn it over on top of the tower. Thump the cup and gently remove it. Build another cup dome for the other tower.
8. With the ruler, square off the sides of each tower by scraping away extra sand.
9. Show your child how to carefully dig a tunnel between the two towers. Let him scoop out a moat around the base of the castle. Without splashing, help him fill the moat with water carried in the pail.
10. It's done. Snap a photo of it and the builders before the waves or other kids come crashing in.

Grow

Have your child estimate how many grains of sand there might be in a handful of sand. How many handfuls might be on the beach where you are? How many in the world? Psalm 139:17-18 says, "How precious to me are your thoughts, O God! How vast is the sum of them! Were I to count them, they would outnumber the grains of sand." God has so many precious thoughts about us, we can't even imagine!

ℯ ℯ ℯ

39

Pedal Pentathlon

Are the kids looking for something to do? Let them "spin their wheels."

Gather
- Long driveway or empty parking lot
- Chalk
- Markers such as plastic cups, milk cartons, or tin cans filled with dirt
- Large coffee cans
- Bicycles
- Bicycle helmets
- Stopwatch

Zigzag Drag Race
Ages 7 and up

Go
1. Use chalk to mark a start/finish line and count 50 paces (100 feet) in a straight line. Every two steps (4 feet) place a marker.
2. Have your child mount her bike a few feet from the start line and ride toward the course. Begin timing with a stopwatch as she crosses the start/finish line. She should pass the first cup on the right, the second on the left, weaving her way between the markers.
3. At the last cup, she should turn around and come back, weaving again. Stop timing when she crosses the start/finish line.
4. If she hits a cup or if her foot touches the ground, she is disqualified.
5. Let her try it on a bike with smaller tires. Was it easier for her? Which was the fastest?
6. As she improves, move the markers closer.

Booking It

Ages 7 and up

Go

1. Let your child practice walking with a book on her head. Then ask her to get on her bike and ride around that way.
2. Begin timing. How many seconds can she ride with the book on her head?

Marbled Maze

Ages 7 and up

Go

1. Follow the setup directions for the "Zigzag Drag Race," except use six large coffee cans for markers and set them every eight steps (16 feet) apart.
2. Have your child hold six marbles and zigzag through the course as before, dropping a marble into each can as she passes it. When she is able to ride the course and drop each marble without missing, time her. Accuracy, control, and speed make this a tough challenge.

Racing Finish

Ages 7 and up

Go

1. Set up a path about two paces wide and 50 paces long (100 feet). Draw chalk lines for boundaries, start, and finish.
2. Have your child begin at the start line. She should get on her bike and sprint down the lane as fast as she can.
3. Time her.
4. Next time, instruct her to ride as slowly as possible, without crossing the boundary lines. Time her again.
5. Ask her which speed is more difficult.

Straight as an Arrow

Ages 7 and up

Go

1. Draw two parallel lines 6 inches apart and about 10 paces(20 feet) long. Put markers along the sides.
2. Time your child as she rides her bike through the markers without knocking any over.
3. See if she can improve her time.

Grow

If your neighborhood has lots of kids with bikes, go to the library and find the rules for bicycle polo. Ask your church or school if you can use the parking lot for a few hours one afternoon and host a polo game.

℮ ℮ ℮

40

The Buck Starts Here

Ages 8 and up

Here are eight ways to earn money in your neighborhood.

1. **Clean cars:** Your kids will need a hose, bucket, soap, rags, sponges, a cardboard sign announcing the location and cost, a place to wash, and the key ingredient—water. Your neighbors need only bring their cars.
2. **Prance with a pooch:** Let your children offer to walk friendly dogs in the neighborhood on a regular schedule.
3. **Do outside chores:** Get your kids raking leaves, weeding gardens, or mowing lawns.
4. **Run errands:** Take your child with you when you go shopping, to the cleaners, the post office, the video store, etc. He can pick up or drop off items for neighbors at the same time.
5. **Host a garage sale:** Open your garage to the neighbors. Let your kids sell stuff on consignment for the neighbors if they agree that your kids get to keep 20 percent of the money earned.
6. **Start a plant nursery:** Teach your child how to grow "spider plants," coleus or "piggybacks." Let her set up a nursery in the backyard and sell the mature plants.
7. **Get picky:** Find out which neighbors have more fruit than they can use. Let your children offer to pick the fruit and clean up the mess in return for some of the food. Make baked goods with it and sell it for a profit.
8. **Appeal to corn nuts:** Plant Indian corn or gourds during the summer to sell in the fall.

Grow

Make sure your child understands that part of the fun of having money is giving it away. If she has that idea before she starts earning, the anticipation will make giving become exciting. "God loves a cheerful giver" (2 Corinthians 9:7).

ᘯ ᘯ ᘯ

41

Getting Out

Ages 4 and up
by Becky Foster Still

Here's how to bring more of the outdoors to your day-to-day activities.

Whatever you're doing, do it outside.
If the weather is decent, there's no reason to stay in your house to pay bills, look through the mail, or catch up on your correspondence. Set up a table outside to do your work while the kids play with their outdoor toys. If you have a cordless phone with sufficient range, make these phone calls outside, too. You may find you're not interrupted as often.

Have dinner (or lunch or breakfast) outside.
Don't wait for perfect weather to have a meal alfresco. If it's a little chilly, bundle up. If it's hot, wear your bathing suits and spray one another with water bottles. If you live in an apartment with no backyard, why not set up a card table in a breezeway or other common area? You'll probably meet some new neighbors you never knew before. Then there's the all-time favorite in my family—take a picnic to our local park.

Bring out a radio and get moving.
Combine fresh air with some physical movement and you've got the perfect antidote for parental stress. With a little music and a lot of kid energy, you can hold your own five-minute aerobics class in the backyard, patio, or balcony. Reach up and pluck stars from the sky. See who can do the most jumping jacks. Invite your children to make up their own exercises. Or just dance, dance, dance!

Play games.
Siblings of different ages and interests will almost always enjoy playing outside games together. Try classics like follow the leader, tag, or hide-and-seek. Have each child act out a particular animal while others guess. Or set up a simple treasure hunt in your yard or other outdoor area, hiding a toy and telling your hunters when they're hot or cold. Then have them set up their own treasure hunt for each other.

Let your little artists make a creative mess outside.
If the activity involves sticky or inky fingers, I always set it up outside. Not only is the mess easier for Mom to deal with, but the open air seems to encourage a child's creativity as he or she paints, stamps with ink pads, or makes interesting play clay concoctions.

Go for a walk.
Take a stroll around the block and make a game out of it. See who can be the first to spot a red car, a black cat, or something that starts with Z. Bring a bag and a magnifying glass and take the time to look for interesting bugs, leaves, and rocks along the way. Sing a song and march. If you're more ambitious, dust off those bikes or skates and really work off some energy.

Grow

So often it seems easier to stay indoors, plugging away at the everyday stuff that needs to be done. But when we remind ourselves to open the door and get out for a bit, we're nearly always renewed and energized. Being outside brings us face-to-face with the wonder and beauty of God's creation—right in our own backyard. This summer, think about adopting an "open door" policy at your home.

SECTION NINE

Recipes

42

Bible Bites

Ages 4 and up
adapted from a recipe by Colleen Dente

Now is the time to let your children play with their food.

Gather
(You'll need some of the things on this list, but certainly not all of them.)
- Lettuce leaves
- Tomato slices
- Carrots—rounds, sticks, and grated
- Cheese—slices and grated
- Raisins
- Bread slices
- Celery sticks
- Cucumber slices
- Olives
- Mandarin oranges
- Grapes
- Pumpkin seeds
- Shredded coconut
- Fruit halves and slices: apples, pears, peaches, etc.
- Peanut butter
- Jelly
- Alfalfa or bean sprouts
- Cottage cheese
- Whipped cream
- Stick pretzels
- Squeeze bottle mustard
- Squeeze bottle ketchup
- Marshmallows, large and small
- Chow mein noodles

Go
1. Help your child decide on a Bible animal or character to make with the snack foods. (See list below or create an idea of your own.)
2. Start with the body or head (a lettuce leaf or piece of fruit) and begin the creation on a paper plate.
3. Use the rest of the foods for legs, arms, hair, eyes, teeth, clothes, etc. (The peanut butter makes great glue.)
4. Add some tuna salad and a glass of milk for a nutritious meal.

Food-friendly Bible characters, animals, and objects

1. Lion of Judah: pear half for head, grated carrots or cheese for mane, raisin eyes, pumpkin-seed teeth.
2. Locusts: celery sticks and cucumbers work great for the body parts; raisin eyes and bean sprouts for antennae.
3. Moses: grated mozzarella cheese for hair, tomato-slice face, lettuce leaf for clothes, pretzels or carrots for arms and legs.
4. Lamb of God: two scoops of cottage cheese, cucumber slices for ears, raisin eyes.
5. Frog: cottage cheese with a little green food coloring, olives or grapes for eyes, celery leaves for legs.
6. Ship: slice of bread for bottom, toothpick mast, cheese triangles for a sail.
7. Chariot: celery stuffed with peanut butter, carrot rounds stuck on with toothpicks for wheels.
8. Joseph and coat of many colors: make a man using fruit for the head and carrots for limbs; his jacket will be a slice of bread with stripes of mustard and ketchup squeezed on it.
9. Rabbit: pear for the base, whipped cream on top of the pear, apple-slice ears, raisin eyes, shredded coconut for the fur.
10. Fish: hard-boiled egg with a wedge cut out for the mouth, raisins for eyes, cucumber slices for side fins, carrot rounds trimmed to triangles for a tail and top fin.

Grow

What other Bible foods can you make? If you come up with a good idea, send it to *Clubhouse* magazine, Colorado Springs, CO 80995. In Canada, mail it to Focus on the Family, P.O. Box 9800, Stn. Terminal, Vancouver, BC V6B 4G3. Be sure to include your name, age, and complete address.

ℰ ℰ ℰ

43

Popsicle Possibilities

Here are two recipes for licks on a stick.

Orange-Sicles

Ages 4 and up
by Jonathan Baptist

Gather
- 2 cups water
- 3 ounces orange gelatin mix

- $^1/_2$ cup sugar
- 2 cups orange juice
- Small paper cups
- Craft sticks

Go

1. Boil the water in a saucepan.
2. Dissolve the sugar and gelatin in the water.
3. Once they are dissolved, remove from heat and pour in the orange juice.
4. Let your child help you fill the paper cups (don't overfill) and put them in the freezer.
5. After two hours, let your child insert a craft stick into each cup. (Or if you can't wait two hours, you can cover the top with plastic wrap and insert the stick. The plastic will keep the stick straight.)
6. Freeze overnight.

Rainbow Refreshment

Ages 4 and up

Gather

- Juices of different colors
- Paper cups
- Plastic wrap or aluminum foil
- Craft sticks

Go

Let your child help with as many of these steps as you can.

1. Pour $^1/_2$ cup of one flavor juice into each cup.
2. Freeze until the juice is hard.
3. Pour $^1/_2$ cup of another juice flavor into each cup. Cover the cups with plastic wrap and insert sticks through the wrap and into the juice. (The plastic will hold the sticks straight.) Put the cups in the freezer until the juice is hard.
4. Alternate adding juice and freezing it until the cups are full.
5. Peel off the paper cups and plastic wrap.

Grow

Be sure your child shares his frozen treats, because getting along with others is cool.

ᘓ   ᘓ   ᘓ

44

Confession Cake

Ages 7 and up
by Courtney Fraser

This dessert can sweeten up bad attitudes in just one bite.

Gather
- 1 large box cake mix
- Cooking utensils (bowl, spatula, mixer, etc.)
- 9- by 13-inch baking pan
- 1 can light-colored frosting
- 1 tube of dark-colored frosting with a thin tip for writing

Go
1. Make the cake with your children according to the directions on the box.
2. After it has cooled, let your children add the light-colored frosting.
3. Read James 5:16 to your family: "Confess your sins to each other and pray for each other so that you may be healed."
4. After discussing the verse, making apologies, and asking forgiveness, have each child write a word or phrase with the dark frosting on the cake that represents something he has done wrong, for example: teasing, angry words, pushing, not sharing, disobedience, impatience. (Mom or Dad, be sure you write something, too!)
5. Cut the cake, and let everyone enjoy it.

Grow
Make sure your child "eats his words" to represent the fact that Jesus takes away his sins when he asks for forgiveness.

ᘓ   ᘓ   ᘓ

45

Cool Chocolate Cookies

Ages 4 and up
by Adam Smith

Already too baked by the sun to turn on the oven? Try these no-bake treats.

Gather
- 2 cups white sugar
- $^1/_2$ cup cocoa
- $^1/_2$ cup milk
- $^1/_2$ cup margarine, melted in the microwave
- $^1/_2$ cup peanut butter
- $2^1/_2$ cups uncooked quick oats
- $^1/_2$ cup shredded coconut or chopped nuts
- 1 teaspoon vanilla
- Waxed paper

Go
1. Help your child measure and pour into a saucepan the sugar, cocoa, milk, and margarine.
2. Heat until boiling, stirring so the milk won't scald.
3. Let your child add peanut butter, oatmeal, coconut or nuts, and vanilla.
4. Blend well with a wooden spoon.
5. Together, drop batter by spoonfuls onto waxed paper.
6. Let it set until firm.

Grow

These cookies make great gifts for others in your church or neighborhood. For the finishing touch, put them in a "Stick-to-It Basket," directions on page 136.

ℰ ℰ ℰ

46

Ice Cream Dream

Ages 6 and up

Create your own individual ice cream machine out of a milk carton and soup can.

Gather
- $^1/_2$ gallon milk carton
- Soup can with watertight lid
- Crushed ice
- Rock salt
- $^1/_2$ cup half-and-half
- 4 teaspoons sugar
- $^1/_2$ teaspoon vanilla
- Metal spoon

Go

1. Put the spoon, soup can, and its lid in the freezer. For best results, let them sit overnight; if you're in a hurry, an hour minimum.
2. Cut off and discard the top half of the milk carton.
3. Let your child add a $1/2$-inch layer of ice and salt to the bottom of the carton.
4. Let her put in the cold can, with the lid on.
5. Help her fill the carton around the can with ice and rock salt (four parts ice to one part salt).
6. Remove the lid of the soup can, and add the half-and-half, sugar, and vanilla.
7. Let her stir the mixture with a cold spoon for 7 to 10 minutes, until the ice cream has frozen.
8. Top with her favorite flavors, fruits, or nuts.

Grow

By adding salt to the ice water, the water gets colder. The saltwater around the can is even colder than the ice. That's why churned ice cream gets thicker and creamier than the same ingredients just tossed into the freezer. Want to learn more about the properties of salt? Try "Ice Fishing" on page 59.

47

Smile Surprise

Ages 4 and up
by Anita Martin

Here's a quick snack your kids can really sink their teeth into.

Gather
- Red apple
- Peanut butter
- Mini-marshmallows

Go

1. Cut the apple into eight even slices.
2. Let your child spread peanut butter on one side of each piece.
3. Let him stick marshmallows into the peanut butter as teeth.
4. Put two pieces together, and it looks like a mouth.

Grow

While snacking, make a plan with your child to make someone smile today. Think up a special day-brightener for a friend, neighbor, church member, or relative.

48

Solar Tea

Ages 4 and up

Brew up fun with some sweet iced tea.

Gather
- Tea bags; orange spice herbal tea makes a great-tasting tea without caffeine
- Large glass jar
- Ice
- Sugar
- Lemon or orange slices

Go
1. Let your child fill the glass jar with water and place a few tea bags inside. It's usually one tea bag for every six ounces of water.
2. Put the jar outside in a sunny place and let the heat from the sun brew the tea.
3. When the tea is light brown (three to six hours later), help your child scoop the tea bags out and pour the tea into glasses filled with ice.
4. Add some sugar (to taste) and a slice of lemon or orange.

Grow
As you sit back and enjoy a glass of tea with your child, take turns thanking the Lord for things that begin with *T*. Start with "*Today*"!

49

Fruit Leather

Ages 7 and up

Dry your own fruit roll-up made with sweet summer fruit.

Gather
- 2 cups chopped summer fruit such as peaches, plums, nectarines, or strawberries
- 1 tablespoon honey
- $1/_2$ teaspoon lemon juice

- Cookie sheet
- Plastic wrap

Go

1. Puree the fruit in a blender or food processor until it's a thick liquid.
2. Pour the fruit into a bowl and let your child add the honey and lemon juice.
3. Help your child spread plastic wrap lightly over the cookie sheet and tape it down.
4. Pour the fruit mixture onto the cookie sheet, and let your child spread it until it's about $1/_4$ inch thick.
5. Ask your child to pick a spot outside in the bright sunlight. Put the pan there and let it dry for two or three days.
6. Each night bring the pan inside and cover it. Check to see if you need to turn the fruit over to allow it to dry faster.
7. When the fruit is dry, roll it up in plastic wrap and store it in the refrigerator.

Grow

During the three days the fruit is drying, help your child memorize the "fruits of the spirit" found in Galatians 5:22: "love, joy, peace, patience, kindness, goodness, faithfulness, gentleness, and self-control." Pin these words up around the house on pieces of construction paper cut out in fruit shapes. (Your family members will especially need self-control so they don't eat up the fruit before it's ready!)

50

Sun-Up Slushes

Ages 4 and up

Surprise your kids for breakfast with these yummy drinks.

Passion for Pineapple

Ages 6 and up

Gather
- 1 20-ounce can crushed pineapple in juice
- $1^1/_2$ cups white sugar
- 3 cups water, or thereabouts

Go

1. Drain the pineapple juice into a large measuring cup and add enough water to make 3 cups total.

2. Pour into a saucepan.

3. Add the sugar to the juice, then heat the mixture so it begins to boil.

4. Turn down the heat and simmer for five minutes. Stir occasionally.

5. Let cool until it reaches room temperature, then stir in the crushed pineapple.

6. Pour the mixture into a 13- by 9-inch baking pan and freeze overnight.

7. Before serving the next morning, let the mixture stand at room temperature for 15 to 30 minutes.

8. Put chunks of the frozen concoction into a blender and mix until it's almost smooth (small pieces of the pineapple should remain).

9. Pour the mixture into cups and serve. Makes about 5 cups.

Fruit Smoothies

Ages 4 and up
by Julia Shingleton

Gather
- 1 frozen, peeled banana
- $1/2$ cup assorted chopped fruits
- 1 teaspoon vanilla flavoring
- $1^1/2$ cups orange juice

Go
1. Blend all ingredients in a blender until smooth and creamy.
2. Serve.

Maple Milkshake

Ages 4 and up
by Matthew Snyder

Gather
- 4 scoops ice cream
- 2 teaspoons maple flavoring
- 2 cups milk

Go
1. Combine in a blender and puree.
2. Make six servings.

Grow

Since you got the morning off to a cheery start, why not keep it that way? As a family, make a vow to work out any problems or disagreements before sunset. Ephesians 4:26 says, "Do not let the sun go down while you are still angry."

51

Berry-Good Dessert

Ages 4 and up
by Brandon Smith

Got an abundance of berries? Whip them up in this recipe.

Gather
- 2 cups blackberries, strawberries, or any other ripe berry
- 1 16-ounce container of whipped topping, thawed
- 3 tablespoons sugar
- 3 tablespoons honey
- 1 8-ounce container of plain yogurt

Go
1. Puree the berries in a blender.
2. Let your child mix the berries with the whipped topping in a large bowl.
3. Help her add the sugar, honey, and yogurt. Blend completely.
4. Let the mixture chill in refrigerator for at least two hours before serving.

Grow
While you are waiting for the berries to chill, call two neighbors and invite them over to share dessert and a game. See pages 13 to 28 for some entertaining ideas.

52

Home Sweet Home

Ages 6 and up

Being stuck at home can be a treat if you're making this candy cottage.

Gather
- Small shoe box (less than 8 inches long)
- Poster board
- Tape and glue
- 1 empty paper towel tube
- 2 packages (7.2 ounces each) white frosting mix

- 1 cup powdered sugar
- 6 to 8 cups popped corn
- $^1/_2$ cup melted butter
- 1 3-ounce package red gelatin
- 1 3-ounce package green gelatin
- 1 tube chocolate decorating icing with plastic tip
- 1 box graham crackers
- Assorted candies

Go

1. Construct a house with the shoebox, tape, glue, and poster board.
2. To make a chimney, cut a hole in the roof and slide the paper towel tube into it. Glue it down.
3. Toss the popped corn with melted butter. Divide the corn into two bowls. Sprinkle red gelatin powder over the popcorn in one bowl, and toss it again to coat the popcorn evenly with gelatin. Do the same thing with the green gelatin powder and the other bowl of popcorn.
4. Make the white frosting mix according to the directions. Beat in the powdered sugar to make the frosting stiffer.
5. Let your child cover the cardboard house with a coat of frosting.
6. Help him stick the colored popcorn and candies into the frosting to cover the walls of the house.
7. He can use more frosting and attach the graham crackers to make shingles for the roof.
8. Use chocolate icing to outline the door and windows.

Grow

Psalm 127:1 says, "Unless the LORD builds the house, its builders labor in vain." Ask your child what the most important part of building a house is. Together list all the ways your family's house is "built" on biblical foundations. Brainstorm ways you can make your family's spiritual house even stronger.

53

Bear Biscuits

Ages 4 and up

These tasty rolls will satisfy a growling tummy.

Gather

- 10 to 12 refrigerator biscuits
- Sesame seeds or sunflower seeds
- Raisins or dried cranberries

Go

1. Take eight biscuits from the package.
2. Let your child separate and roll each portion of dough into a ball.
3. She can then roll the eight balls into the seeds.
4. Place them on a greased cookie sheet, and flatten them slightly into circles.
5. Use the rest of the dough to make ears. Your child can roll the biscuit ears in the seeds and press them onto the bears' heads.
6. Add raisin or cranberry eyes and noses.
7. Bake at 400° for 8 to 10 minutes.

Grow

There is a Bible story about the prophet Elisha being teased by some young men (2 Kings 2:23-25). The youths were jeering at him and calling him "baldhead." God allowed some nearby bears to bolt from the woods and chase the young men away. During dinner as you eat the biscuit bears, tell your child this story. Discuss why calling people names displeases God.

54

Taffy Tug

Ages 7 and up

Your kids will love pulling off this traditional candy recipe.

Gather
- $1^1/_2$ cups sugar
- $^1/_2$ cup light corn syrup
- $^1/_4$ cup water
- 2 tablespoons butter
- $^1/_2$ teaspoon peppermint extract
- Pinch of salt
- Red food coloring

Go

1. Let your child help you combine all the ingredients except the food coloring in a large, heavy saucepan.
2. Heat the mixture, stirring constantly.
3. Keep heating it until a bit of the mixture dropped in cold water forms a ball (260°on a candy thermometer).
4. Pour the taffy onto a buttered plate.

5. As the taffy cools, fold the edges toward the center. When it's cool enough to pick up, divide the taffy in half. Add red food coloring to one half and let your child knead it until the taffy is pink.
6. Butter your hands and ask your child to do the same. Take a handful of taffy and knead, pull and stretch it with your partner. If it gets too sticky, put more butter on your hands.
7. With your child, pull the taffy into long, wide strips.
8. Help your child cut the strips into 2-inch pieces.
9. He can take a piece of pink taffy and a piece of white and twist them together.
10. To finish, wrap the finished taffy in small pieces of waxed paper or cellophane, twisting the ends to seal them.

Grow

Like the candy cane, this red-and-white taffy carries a visual reminder of Christ's forgiveness. The red represents His blood shed for us on the cross. The white represents His pure, sinless nature.

55

Critter Crackers

Ages 6 and up

During the Dog Days of August, make these biscuits to pamper your pooch.

Gather
- $1/_2$ cup rolled oats
- 2 teaspoons honey
- $1/_2$ teaspoon salt
- $3/_4$ cup whole wheat flour
- $1/_4$ teaspoon baking soda
- $1/_4$ cup butter
- $1/_4$ cup buttermilk
- $1/_8$ teaspoon vanilla
- 1 teaspoon cinnamon

Go
1. Preheat the oven to 400°.
2. Place the oats in a blender and spin them until they're ground to a fine flour. Let your child place the ground oats in a large mixing bowl and add the honey, salt, flour, and baking soda. Mix well.
3. Help your child cut the butter into small pieces and add it to the mixture. Your child can then add the buttermilk, vanilla, and cinnamon; mix the dough well.

4. Together, roll the dough out on a floured surface. Make sure it is thin and even. Let your child cut it with animal-shaped cookie cutters.

5. Place the cookies on a grease-free baking sheet and bake for 10 to 12 minutes until the crackers are golden brown. Let them cool on cooling racks.

Grow

Being gentle with animals is good training for developing patience and kindness to people, too. Proverbs 12:10 says, "A righteous man cares for the needs of his animal, but the kindest acts of the wicked are cruel."

ℰ   ℰ   ℰ

56

Gooey Granola Bars

Ages 6 and up

These goodies make a nutritious treat for hiking or camping.

Gather
- $1/_4$ cup sugar
- $1/_4$ cup margarine
- $1/_3$ cup honey
- $1/_2$ teaspoon ground cinnamon
- 1 cup diced dried fruits and raisins
- $1 1/_2$ cups whole-grain wheat flake cereal
- 1 cup quick cooking oats
- $1/_2$ cup sliced almonds

Go
1. Mix sugar, margarine, honey, and cinnamon in a saucepan.
2. Ask an adult to help you heat the mixture over medium heat, stirring it continuously. Keep heating the mixture until it boils for one minute.
3. Stir in the dried fruits and raisins.
4. Add wheat cereal, oats, and almonds.
5. Press the mixture in a greased pan.
6. Let it cool and cut it into bars.

Grow

Put some of these in your "homeless bag"—items to give away to those in need. See "Heart for the Homeless" on page 6 for more ideas.

e e e

57

Pretzel Pleasers

Ages 6 and up

Homemade pretzels feed the heart as well as the stomach.

Gather
- $^1/_2$ teaspoon dry yeast
- 3 tablespoons warm water (105°)
- $^1/_2$ teaspoon sugar
- $^1/_2$ cup flour
- 1 egg
- Salt

Go

1. Have your kids wash their hands.
2. Sprinkle the yeast into the warm water.
3. Stir it until it dissolves.
4. Add the sugar. Add the flour.
5. Stir this, then knead it.
6. Cut the dough into four pieces.
7. Roll each piece between your hands until it makes a "worm" about 10 to 12 inches long.
8. Put the dough on a greased cookie sheet and shape it into a pretzel, as shown.
9. Press the ends together.
10. Brush each pretzel with beaten egg.
11. Sprinkle them with salt.
12. Bake at 425° for about 15 minutes or until light brown.

Grow

The word "pretzel" comes from Latin, meaning "little reward." A pretzel was originally a cross enclosed in a circle. It was customary to give children the treat as a reward for saying their prayers. Why not keep the tradition going?

58

Straw Shack Snack

Ages 4 and up

Build a house out of "straw" and watch your children wolf it down.

Gather
- 1 large wheat biscuit (Shredded Wheat)
- 1 jar marshmallow cream
- Raisins

Go
1. Let your child crumble up the wheat cereal biscuit.
2. Help her spoon in the marshmallow mixture one spoonful at a time until the mixture is sticky enough to hold its shape.
3. Teach her how to shape the mixture into a house.
4. Let her stick in raisins for doors and windows.
5. Put the house in a bowl and pour milk over it.
6. Let your child gobble the house up.

Grow
There are several similarities between the tale of the three pigs and Jesus' parable about the houses built on sand and rock. While your child is eating her snack, read the story found in Matthew 7:24-27.

59

Cookie Bouquet

Ages 6 and up
by Marianne K. Hering

A flowery surprise that tastes as good as it looks!

Gather
- $1/_8$-inch thick dowels or very thin craft sticks
- 3 cups flour

- 1 cup butter or margarine, softened
- 1 cup granulated sugar
- 2 teaspoons baking powder
- 1 teaspoon vanilla
- 2 cups powdered sugar
- 2 to 3 tablespoons hot water
- Cookie cutters
- Waxed paper
- Food coloring
- Green construction paper
- Scissors
- Nontoxic white glue
- Cooking utensils (bowls, spatula, mixer, cookie sheets, knives, etc.)

Go

1. Preheat the oven to 400°.
2. Cut dowels into 12- to 14-inch sections. If you use all the dough, you will need about 30 dowel sections.
3. In an electric mixer, cream the granulated sugar and butter. Next, add the egg and vanilla. Blend well.
4. Add the baking powder to the flour. Mix 2 cups flour mixture into the butter batter.
5. Mix in the last cup of flour by hand; the dough should be stiff. You may have to squish it all together with your fingers. Do not chill.
6. Separate the batter into two equal sections. Using just half the dough at a time, roll it into a 6-inch circle. The batter should be $1/4$-inch thick. (Thick is better than too thin.)
7. Let your child cut out flowers with cookie cutters or a cardboard pattern and a butter knife.
    - Lily with bell turned over
    - Daisy with a biscuit cutter or glass to make circles
    - Tulip with the shape above as a pattern
    - Rose with an upside-down heart
    - Butterflies, ducks, or crosses will also look nice in your spring bouquet
8. Each cookie sheet will hold six cookies with long dowels or about nine with shorter dowels or craft sticks. Put three uncooked cookies at each end of a dry, grease-free baking sheet. Gently push the dowel or craft stick into the center of the cookie as for a stem, pushing the stick as far to the top as possible. (If you mess up, not to worry. Just gather the dough and roll it out again.)
9. Bake for six to eight minutes. (Don't worry about the wood burning. It won't combust in a 400° oven.)
10. Remove the cookies immediately with a spatula. Place them on a sheet of waxed paper. Do not attempt to pick them up by the stem until they are completely cool.
11. Make the icing by mixing the powdered sugar and hot water. Add one or two more drops of hot water if it is too dry.
12. Separate the icing into little bowls and add drops of food coloring. Mix.

13. When they are cool, let your child decorate the flower cookies with icing.
14. Add leaves cut out of green construction paper. Your child can glue or tape them on.
15. To finish the bouquet, wrap it in cellophane decorator paper and tie it with a bow. The bouquet can also be displayed in a heavy vase. (They don't need water!)

Grow

Use this bouquet as a thank-you gift for your child's Sunday school teacher.

ᙍ ᙍ ᙍ

60

Brown Bag Bonanza

Ages 4 and up

Spruce up an on-the-go lunch with these kid-friendly ideas.

1. **Banana and peanut-butter sandwich:** Spread peanut butter on a slice of banana bread. Top it with another slice.
2. **Celery palms:** Rinse two or three pieces of celery. Cut each piece lengthwise into sticks. From one end of each stick, make several slits halfway down. Soak the celery in cold water for an hour until the "leaves" curl.
3. **Jungle mix:** In a plastic bag, mix granola, raisins, and dried fruit. Shake the bag well. You can also add your child's favorite dried cereal for extra crunch.
4. **Tortilla treat:** Mix chunks of chicken with ranch dressing, chopped cucumber, and shredded cheese. Wrap the salad in a tortilla.
5. **Carrot curls:** Wash and peel carrots. Then use the peeler to make long, thick curls. (If they're not curly enough, try curling them around your finger and securing with a toothpick.) Soak them in water until you're ready to pack them in a lunch.
6. **Cinnamon crispies:** In a frying pan, brown a flour tortilla in a little butter. Pat it dry on a paper towel. Then sprinkle the tortilla with cinnamon and sugar. Break it into bite-sized pieces.
7. **Vegetable confetti:** Mix short carrots and celery sticks, cherry tomatoes, and small pieces of broccoli in a plastic bag. Send along some salad dressing for dipping.
8. **Peanut popcorn:** Mix $1/4$ cup sugar, $1/4$ cup milk, and $1/2$ cup peanut butter in a pan. Cook until it boils. Pour it over 4 cups of popped popcorn and mix well.
9. **Tuna-salad boats:** Cut an apple in half. Remove the core and seeds. Drain a can of tuna and mix it with some mayonnaise and a pinch of salt and pepper. Fill the hole in the apple with some of the tuna salad. Top the boat with a sail made of cheese.
10. **Crazy cucumber:** Decorate a cucumber by attaching other vegetables with toothpicks. Radishes for eyes and nose, a smile-shaped slice of turnip for a mouth, mushrooms for ears, and short, thin carrot sticks for hair.—*Stephanie Stol*

Grow

Remember the boy who shared his lunch with Jesus? Five thousand people were fed that day (John 6) with five barley loaves and two fish. Be sure to pack extra so your child can practice practical giving.

ℰ ℰ ℰ

61

Dirt Dessert

Ages 4 and up

This treat will worm its way into your child's heart and mouth!

Gather
- Chocolate pudding
- 1 package chocolate sandwich cookies, crushed and crumbled
- 8 clear plastic cups
- Gummy worms
- 8 plastic spoons or straws
- Construction paper

Go
1. Help your child make the pudding according to the package directions.
2. Mix half of the cookie crumbles into the pudding and let your child stir. Chill.
3. Your child can put a tablespoon of crumbs into the bottom of each cup and fill the cups with the pudding mixture.
4. Sprinkle the rest of the crumbles on top. Chill for one hour.
5. Let your child arrange the gummy worms on top.
6. Together, make construction-paper flowers and glue them to the straws. "Plant" the straws in the cups.

Grow

This decadent dessert is perfect for a celebration. Make it for special occasion like a baseball game victory, a sibling's return from camp, or the grand finale of a garage sale.

62

Fruity Fizz

Ages 4 and up

This tasty drink is a favorite at Whit's End.

Gather
- 1 cup sherbet
- $^1/_4$ cup fresh fruit, chopped
- 1 cup lemon-lime soda

Go

1. Place all the ingredients in a blender. Blend until smooth.
2. Serve with straws.

Grow

While you drink your "Fruity Fizz," tune into "Adventures in Odyssey" to add some drama to your summer. For stations and times, call 1-800-A-FAMILY (232-6459) to request a radio schedule.

63

Sunshine Sizzle

Ages 6 and up

Cook lunch with this solar-powered oven made from an oatmeal carton.

Gather
- 1 small oatmeal container, empty
- Foil
- Long skewer
- Black nontoxic paint (optional)
- Mirror (optional)
- Hot dog

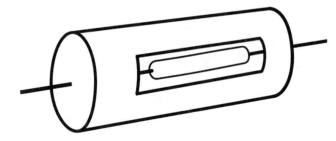

Go

1. Cut a 8- by 4-inch section out of the side of the oatmeal container.
2. Help your child line the container with foil, shiny side out.
3. Push the skewer through the center of what was the top of the oatmeal carton. Slide the hot dog on the skewer, and then push the tip of the skewer out the bottom. The hot dog should be positioned in the center of the "oven."
4. Optional: Let your child paint the dull side of some aluminum foil black and allow it to dry. Help him wrap the foil, black side out, around the hot dog.
5. Put the cooker outside and turn the opening toward the sun. You may need to tilt it in place with some rocks.
6. Optional: To add more heat, help your child position a mirror to reflect on the hot dog.
7. If it's a hot, sunny day, your child's hot dog should be ready in about a half hour.

Grow

What other things can you cook in the sun? Try warming marshmallows or vegetables on the skewer. If you're very brave, experiment with frying an egg. Invite one of your neighborhood children to share the solar lunch, or let them do their own under your supervision.

64

Lemon Drop Cookies

Ages 7 and up

Enjoy these tart treats with a glass of lemonade.

Gather
- 1 cup butter or margarine
- 1 cup sugar
- 2 eggs
- 3 cups flour
- 1 teaspoon baking soda
- 6-ounce can frozen lemonade concentrate, thawed
- $^1/_2$ cup powdered sugar

Go

Let your child help with measuring and pouring.

1. In a large bowl, beat together the butter and sugar until the mixture is fluffy.
2. Add the eggs and mix well.
3. In another bowl, stir together the flour and baking soda. Add half of the flour mixture to the butter mixture and beat well.

4. Pour $^1/_2$ cup of the lemonade concentrate into the dough and stir. Then add the rest of the flour and mix until the dough is well blended.
5. Let your child drop spoonfuls of dough onto a grease-free cookie sheet about 2 inches apart.
6. Bake the cookies at 375° for 10 to 12 minutes, or until the cookies are light brown on top.
7. Let the cookies cool completely. Then let your child brush each one with some of the leftover lemonade concentrate and sprinkle with some powdered sugar.

Grow

Take at least six cookies to a neighbor you've never met before. Enclose a copy of the recipe. On the other side of the recipe card, include a "recipe" for a bountiful life: **Gather:** Your heart, God's grace, and promises from the Bible. **Go:** 1. Read the Gospel of John found in the New Testament. 2. Confess your failings to God and those you have hurt. Ask God and people to forgive you. 3. Ask God to live in you through the Holy Spirit. 4. Do good to others and steer clear of things Jesus wouldn't do.

SECTION TEN

Crafts

65

Just-in-Case Vase

Ages 6 and up
by Renee Martinoski

Showcase flowers all year long in an empty potato chip can.

Gather
- 1 empty potato chip can or other long, thin can
- Aluminum foil
- Ribbon
- Stickers
- Florist foam
- Long or medium-stemmed flowers

Go
1. Let your child tape aluminum foil to the outside of the can.
2. Help her decorate with ribbon.
3. Next, she will put stickers on the foil.
4. Place florist foam inside can and add water.
5. Push larger flowers into the foam first. Fill in with smaller flowers. Have fun and don't forget to water!

Grow
Decorate these vases with crosses and doves and donate them to your church to use as sanctuary decorations. Make several of them just in case you need to bring flowers to a sick friend or to celebrate a new birth.

ℰ ℰ ℰ

66

One-of-a-Kind Critters

Ages 6 and up

Use paints and fingerprints to create these unique animal designs.

Gather
- Tempera paints
- White paper
- Paper plates or pie tins
- Newspaper or paper towels

Go

    1. After protecting your workspace with plastic or newspaper, pour a glob of paint on the paper plates or pie tins. Use one color for each container. Add water if the paint is too thick.

    2. Have your child practice dipping hand and fingers into the paint and then pressing them on the newspaper. Use bent or curled fingers for some shapes. Note the different shapes each part of the hand makes.

    3. Once your child has the hang of it, have him make animal designs on the white paper. Let him make pretend animals and real ones.

    4. Add a friendly message on each paper and give them away to friends or neighbors. Each person's fingerprints are unique, so every critter made is one of a kind.

Grow

Discuss the creation story found in Genesis 1:24-25. Ask your child what it feels like to create a "new" animal on the paper. Remind him that God's creation was "good" and so is his.

ℰ   ℰ   ℰ

67

Armor of God

Ages 4 and up
by Sheila Seifert

Get ready for battle—spiritual battle—by making the "Armor of God."

Gather
- Roll of duct tape
- 40 to 100 or so juice can lids (and bottoms if you can get the cardboard out)
- Belt with a buckle
- Scissors
- Piece of cardboard

Go (for the Breastplate of Righteousness)

    1. Cut three 10-inch pieces of duct tape and place them sticky side up.

    2. Put four juice can lids on each piece of tape.

    3. Cut four 9-inch pieces of tape. Use these to tape together the already taped lids.

    4. Cut three 9-inch pieces of tape. Put three juice can lids on each of these strips of tape.

    5. With three more 9-inch pieces of tape, fasten together juice lids in a grid-shape as shown.

    6. Take two pieces of duct tape 18 inches long. Stick four lids to each strip with 3 inches of tape sticking out each side. These are the shoulder straps for the vest.

    7. Attach the shoulder straps to the 4 x 4 panels.

8. Reinforce the back with more duct tape if you want.
9. Then let your child slip on his Breastplate of Righteousness. Secure it with a belt for the "belt of truth."

Go (for the Shield of Faith)
1. Follow the above steps 1-3.
2. Then cut a piece of cardboard the same size as the juice-lid grid.
3. Tape the cardboard to the back of the shield.
4. Twist several pieces of 9-inch long duct tape together to make a "rope." Tape it to the back of the shield for a holder.

Grow

Want to read more about the "Armor of God"? It is described in Ephesians 6:13-17.

68

Hop-Along Friend

Ages 4 and up

Stage an old-fashioned jumping contest using paper frogs.

Gather
• Green construction paper
• Markers

Go

1. Start with a rectangular 8$\frac{1}{2}$-by-11-inch piece of paper. Green looks the best, of course. Most folds can be made by a kindergartner; however, most children will need help with steps 4 and 5.
2. Fold down the right corner, unfold.
3. Fold down the left corner, unfold.
4. Fold in half, and bring sides in.
5. Push top down.

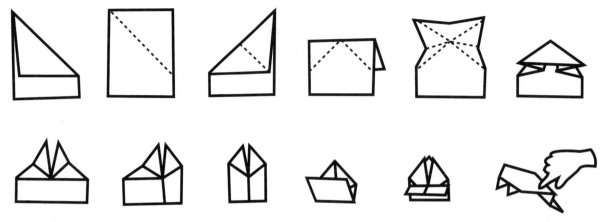

6. Bend flaps up to a point.
7. Fold both sides in.
8. Fold bottom flap up.
9. Then fold down half of the bottom flap.
10. Next fold the two loose triangles down.
11. Draw on eyes.
12. Jump!

Grow

If you make enough paper frogs, your family can pretend amphibians are invading. Read the story of the plagues in Exodus 8:1-15 aloud and ask your child to dramatize the passage using the frogs as props. Make sure you get to the end of the passage where Moses asks God to stop the frogs.

69

Cherry Tree Placemat

Ages 6 and up

This artwork is blooming with good fun.

Gather
- Brown or black ink or tempera paint
- Red and green tempera paints
- Newspaper
- Straw
- White construction paper (computer paper is too thin)
- Sponge
- Scissors
- Clear Con-Tact paper

Go

1. Place a dab of black or brown paint or ink at the bottom center of some newspaper.
2. Give your child a straw. Let him gently blow through the straw and spread the paint upward on the paper. (Add more water if the paint is too thick.) This will form the tree trunk and branches. After you've practiced, do it on the real paper. Let it dry.
3. Cut a wedge of sponge shaped like a leaf. Let your child dip it in the green paint and cover the branches with leaves. Let it dry.
4. Next, let him dip a fingertip in the red paint and put cherries on the tree.
5. Have him sign his name to the paper, and when it is dry, cover the paper with Con-Tact paper.
6. It's now ready to use as a mat at the table.

Grow

Use the placemat at a meal where the focus in on the trees that God has made. Psalm 1 says, "He is like a tree planted by streams of water, which yields its fruit in season…." Discuss with your children how they can be "planted" in God's Word.

70

Jigsaw Puzzle Frame

Ages 4 and up
by Natasha and Amber Giesbrect

This fun photo frame is a perfect fit for any family photo.

Gather
- Heavy cardboard
- Jigsaw puzzle with small pieces
- Glue

Go

1. Cut two pieces of cardboard 8 by 11 inches. In one piece of cardboard, cut a 5- by 7-inch frame opening. (Or adjust to fit any size photo.)
2. Let your child glue the puzzle pieces around the border. Let dry.
3. Glue the second piece of cardboard to the back of the frame at the bottom and side edges only. Leave the top open to slide in the photo.

Grow

This frame makes a great gift for grandparents or other family members. You can glue a magnet to the back and use it on the refrigerator.

ℰ ℰ ℰ

71

Lightning Bug Luminarias

Ages 4 and up

This illuminating idea will shed light on a summer evening *and* on God's nature.

Gather
- Paper bags, assorted sizes
- Hole punch
- Flashlights, one for each bag
- Votive candles and holders (optional)

Go
1. Have each child draw a big cross on a bag.
2. With your help, let each child punch holes around the outline of the cross. In order to do this, you may need to fold the bags.
3. If your child wants to, let him punch out other designs or part of the inside of the cross.
4. Your child can open the bag and place it on your porch or picnic table. Turn on the flashlight and put it inside the bag. Fold the top of the bag closed. (If you are going to be right next to the bag, then use a votive candle. Be sure to put it out if you leave the table. Candles are irresistible to some children.)

Grow
Use the bag as a discussion starter. After dark one night, hide the bag or bags in an out-of-the-way corner(s). Be sure the flashlights are on. Next choose which one of the following verses is appropriate for your child: Matthew 5:14-16, Luke 8:16-18, or 1 John 1:5-7. Mark it with a bookmark as well as 1 John 2:8, which says, "The darkness is passing, and the true light is already shining." Ask your child to find the hidden bag. Read the verses together and discuss how God's spiritual light is like physical light.

ᓚ   ᓚ   ᓚ

72

A Good Sign

Ages 4 and up

Make a nighttime reminder of God's goodness out of a manila folder and some string.

Gather
- File folder, letter or legal size
- Ruler
- Scissors
- Markers
- Yarn, two or three colors
- Glue
- Stickers or glitter
- Hole punch

Go
1. Cut out three rectangles from the file folder: 4 inches by 6 inches, 4 inches by 8 inches, 4 inches by 11 inches.
2. Use markers to color both sides of the rectangles.
3. For the word *GOD,* cut a piece of yarn about the length of the *G.* Do the same for *O* and *D.*
4. Write GOD in glue on the 8-inch rectangle. Let your child press the three pieces of yarn into the glue.
5. Use glue and different colors of yarn to write PROTECTS and ME on the big card and small card.
6. After the glue dries, write GOD and ME on the flip side of those cards. Write LOVES on the flip side of the PROTECTS card.
7. Let your child decorate the cards with glitter, stickers, markers, and bits of colored paper.
8. Punch holes in the middle of the tops and bottoms of the GOD and PROTECTS cards. Punch one hole in the middle of the top of the ME card.
9. Using pieces of yarn, tie the cards together, with two inches of space between each card.
10. Put a long piece of yarn through the top hole in the GOD card and use that yarn to hang the mobile from the ceiling of your child's room.

Grow
Use the mobile as a discussion starter at bedtime. Change the middle card regularly to discuss other truths about God.

e e e

73

Rock-Solid Family

Ages 4 and up

Decorate your own "rock group" with beach stones or those purchased at a garden store.

Gather
- Smooth, flat stones, both large and small
- Acrylic or poster paints
- Paint brushes
- White glue
- Craft sticks
- Paper
- Scissors
- Yarn, spaghetti, fabric scraps, other bric-a-brac

Go
1. Set up a work area and dress your child in art-proof clothes.
2. Let her choose two to five rocks for each person she wants to make. Rocks are used for heads, bodies, and feet.
3. She should start by painting all the bodies white to prime them.
4. Next, she should paint the body parts (face, feet) that will be flesh colored the appropriate shade of tan to dark brown. Also, if she wants arms, she should paint two craft sticks the same shade.
5. When the paint is dry, help her glue the bodies together. The rock people will need to lean against something for support until the glue dries.
6. When they are dry, let her paint faces, hair, clothes, etc.
7. Break the craft sticks in half and glue them on.
8. Add details: Draw or glue on buttons. Make a scarf out of fabric scraps. What about ties, jewelry, or a purse? How would spaghetti or yarn work for hair?
9. Let the glue and paint dry.

Grow
Bet Dad could use a model of your family in his office. Why not make him one for Father's Day?

ℰ ℰ ℰ

74

Bath-Time Tricks

Ages 4 and up
by Barbara Schoonover

Rub-a-dub-dub! Have fun in the tub with homemade paints.

Gather
- Empty foam egg carton
- Scissors
- Liquid soap
- Red, blue, and yellow food coloring
- Stir stick
- Paintbrush

Go
1. To get the mixture just right, you'll need to help both younger and older kids with this craft. Food coloring will not stain most bathroom grout or sealant; however, it is best to do a spot check before use.
2. Cut off the top of the egg carton. Then cut the side with cups in half, leaving six egg cups per side.
3. Add one or two drops of food coloring to each cup. Mix the red, blue, and yellow colors to make six neat shades. Red and yellow make orange. Blue and red make purple. Yellow and blue make green. Add about two tablespoons liquid soap to each cup, filling it 2/3 full.
4. When your child is ready to take a bath, float the foam soap boat in the water. Give her a paintbrush and let her paint herself like a rainbow.
5. When she is done, rinse away the colors with water and save the paint boat for another day of good clean fun.

Grow
After your child has colored her body, use that moment as a humorous illustration to teach your child that the color of a person's skin does not change the person inside. God loves us all, no matter what skin color we have.

ℭ ℭ ℭ

75

Fit to Be Tied

Ages 4 and up

Design a Father's Day card that lets Pop know he's tops.

Gather
- Construction paper
- Wrapping paper
- 3 buttons
- Photo or drawing of your child

Go
1. Fold a piece of construction paper in half lengthwise.
2. Cut two strips of construction paper. Fold them as shown. Glue them to the middle of the folded edge of the paper to make a collar.
3. Cut a tie out of wrapping paper and let your child glue it to the "collar" of your card.
4. Cut a square of construction paper bigger than the photo. Glue three edges of it to the right side of the card to make a pocket.
5. Help your child glue two buttons on the collar, like buttons on a shirt. Be sure to glue one button to the pocket. If the child's dad does not wear a tie, make a shirt that is similar to his work uniform or attire.
6. When the glue is dry, stick a photo of your child inside the pocket of the shirt. If you don't have a photo, let your child draw a self-portrait.

Grow
Help him write a special message to Dad inside the card. You can include one or more of these verses: Psalm 112:1-2, 4, 6; Proverbs 20:7. For more Father's Day ideas, see "Rock-Solid Family" and "Soap on a Rope" on pages 120 and 133.

~ ~ ~

76

Crafts Worth Their Salt

Two traditional crafts that give a different "flavor."

Salty Sceneries

Ages 4 and up

This recipe will "spice up" traditional paints.

Gather
- 1 cup salt
- 1 cup flour
- 2 cups water
- 4 different colors tempera paint, $^1/_2$ cup each color

Go
1. Mix the salt, flour, and water. Divide the mixture into four pie tins.
2. Add $^1/_2$ cup of each color of tempera paint to each tin and mix it in.
3. Let your child paint away. If you know a shut-in, ask your child to paint a landscape for someone who needs some hope on the horizon.

Salt and Letters

Ages 4 and up

This bedroom decoration will help your child know he's "the salt of the earth."

Gather
- 2 cups salt
- 1 cup cornstarch
- $1^1/_4$ cups cold water
- Paper clips

Go
1. Let your child help you mix the salt, cornstarch, and cold water in a saucepan.
2. Heat the dough mixture until it is very thick.
3. Let the dough cool a little. Then let your child squish it between his fingers until it's smooth.

4. Let him use the dough to shape the letters of his name.
5. Press the paper clips into the backs of the letters to make hooks.
6. Let the dough dry until it's hard. Then hang the letters in your child's room as a decoration.

Grow

Read Matthew 5:13, "You are the salt of the earth. But if the salt loses its saltiness, how can it be made salty again?" Discuss why salt is good. (Your body needs it; it makes food taste good; it preserves food.) Ask your child why Jesus wants Christians to be the "salt of the earth." (To be an essential part of God's plan for the world's salvation; to flavor the world with goodness; to preserve the goodness in our culture.)

77

Personal-Sized Piñata

Ages 4 and up
by Shannon Williams

Make mini-piñatas for some party pizzazz.

Gather
- 2 Styrofoam cups
- Individually wrapped candies
- Confetti
- String or yarn
- Sharp pencil
- Glue
- Colored tissue paper
- Streamers

Go
1. Fill one cup with candies and confetti.
2. Punch a hole in the center of the bottom of the other cup. Put one end of the string in the hole and tie it to a piece of candy so the string can't come out of the hole.
3. Glue the cup with the string onto the top of the filled cup. Let it dry overnight.
4. Let your child glue tissue paper and streamers to the cups for decoration.
5. After all the glue dries, hang up the piñata. Blindfold your child and let her whack away.

Grow

You can use these as birthday party favors and include small toys and strips of paper with Bible verses written on them.

ॐ

78
Accessory Assortment

Let your little gems make their own jewelry.

Salvation Bracelet

Ages 4 and up
by Rachel Toscano

Five beads and some string create a daily reminder of Jesus' love.

Gather
- 1 piece of black cord, 14 inches long
- 5 beads, one each of the following colors: black, red, white, green, yellow

Go
1. Take the black cord and tie a knot about 6 inches from one end.
2. Let your child slip the beads on in the order listed above.
3. Tie a knot after the yellow bead.
4. Tie the whole thing on your child's wrist.

Grow
This bracelet is a reminder of Jesus' life, death, and resurrection:
The first knot = Christ's birth
Black bead = sin
Red bead = Christ's blood shed on the cross for our sins
White bead = the purification of our souls after God forgives our sins
Green bead = everlasting life
Yellow bead = heaven
Last knot = Christ's resurrection and new life.
Share the message of God's love using your bracelet.

Bead It

Ages 10 and up
by Kate Edwards

Let this craft string you along your way to making homemade jewelry.

Gather
- Lightweight fishing line

- Scissors
- 3 colors of seed beads
- Small jewelry clasp (optional)

Go

1. Let your child follow these directions. Be on hand for steps 6 and 7.
2. Cut fishing line twice the length of your wrist, neck, ankle, or finger.
3. Tie knots in one end of the string to keep the beads from falling off.
4. Put five beads of the same color on the line. Follow with seven beads of another color.
5. Push the end of the fishing line without the knot through the first bead on the second color. Do not pull tight.
6. Put one bead of the third color on the line, as shown.
7. Thread fishing line through the middle bead of the set of seven beads.
8. Pull tight and you'll have a flower.
9. Repeat steps 3 through 7 until your creation is long enough for your wrist, neck, ankle, or finger. Tie ends together or to each end of a clasp. Cut off extra string.
10. Try other combinations using different numbers of colors or beads.

Natural Necklaces

Ages 8 and up

String some "seed-sational" fashion statements.

Gather

- Assorted dried seeds, beans, and corn kernels
- Bowl of hot water
- Colander
- Heavy thread
- Embroidery needle

Go

This craft requires needlework. Please supervise those younger than 12.

1. Rinse the seeds thoroughly, and soak the seeds overnight in water.
2. Drain the seeds, and pat them dry.
3. Double-thread the needle to the desired length and add 2 inches. (Make sure the necklace will fit over the wearer's head.) Knot the thread an inch or so from the ends to make a tail.
4. Start stringing the seeds in a fun pattern. Stop stringing when there is about an inch left of string from the needle.
5. Cut the needle loose and then knot the ends. Tie the tail and other end together to make your necklace complete.
6. Let necklace dry in a sunny spot for a day or two.

Grow

Encourage your daughter to make friendship bracelets or necklaces for all her school friends. Or include them in care packages for homeless families. If you make the "Salvation Bracelet" (p. 125), be sure you include a note explaining what the colors represent. See the section on "People-Helping Projects" (pages 5-10) for more ideas on ways to share with others.

79

Puppet Buddies

Ages 4 and up

A brown paper bag puppet can make a fantastic friend.

Gather
- Plain, small paper sack
- Markers
- Construction paper
- Scissors
- Glue
- Yarn, buttons, scraps of cloth

Go
1. Give your child a closed paper sack.
2. Show the him where to draw eyes and a nose on what would normally be the bottom of the sack.
3. The puppet's mouth is the fold of the bag. Show your child where to draw an upper lip (along the top edge) and where to draw a bottom lip (below the fold).
4. Give him some yarn, a pair of scissors, and some glue. Show him how to cut and glue yarn to the puppet's head for hair.
5. For ears, let your child cut out semicircles from the construction paper. Help him glue the ears inside the fold.
6. To make arms, let your child fold a piece of construction paper in half. Let him draw an arm with a hand. Now let him cut it out. (Each child will end up with two arms that are the same size.) The arms are glued halfway down the sack inside the middle fold.
7. To give each puppet a colorful shirt, your child can color the bags with markers or cut a shirt out of paper or fabric and glue it on.
8. Put your hand inside a sack and slip your fingers over the fold. Open your hand to make the puppet talk. Make sure your child knows how to operate his puppet pal.
9. Create a puppet theatre by draping a blanket over a couple of chairs.

Grow

Write a short play with your child. Good topics are a lost dog, going to a birthday party, a bully who needs a friend, or a Bible story. Make the puppets he needs to perform the play and invite at least two of his friends over to watch it. Be sure to serve yummy snacks. See "Bible Bites" on page 89 for some creative ideas.

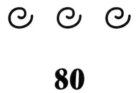

80

Afloat with Fun

These two simple ships sail in the bathtub.

Balloon Boat

Ages 4 and up

Gather
- 1 Styrofoam or plastic plate for each boat
- 1 round balloon for each boat

Go
1. Poke a small hole in the center of the plate.
2. Before blowing up the balloon, push the open end through the hole.
3. Blow up the balloon and knot it.
4. Float the boat in a swimming pool, lake, or bathtub.

Sailing on a Half-Shell

Ages 4 and up

Gather
- Play clay (any non-hardening clay or florist clay)
- Empty walnut shells
- Construction paper
- Glue
- Toothpicks
- Markers or crayons

Go

1. Your child can fill the shell with a ball of clay. Make sure she packs it tightly.
2. Draw a triangle that is shorter than a toothpick on a piece of construction paper and let her cut it out.
3. With the markers, let her color the sail.
4. Glue the sail to the toothpick and let it dry. Or poke the toothpick through the top and bottom.
5. Stick the sail into the clay.
6. Let your child experiment with different shapes and numbers of sails.
7. Put the shell boat in the sink or tub and sail away.

Grow

Are your kids nuts about boats? Read these three Bible stories that offer waves of excitement: Jonah 1, Matthew 14:22-33, Acts 27:13-44.

81

Jump on the Bandwagon

These four musical instruments will bring down the house.

Toot Your Own Horn

Ages 6 and up

Cut and fold this paper whistle and turn ho-hums into whoo-hoos.

Gather
- Piece of paper
- Scissors

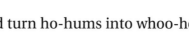

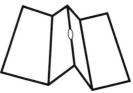

Go

1. Cut a 3-by 5-inch rectangle out of the paper.
2. Fold it in half.
3. Cut two to three small ($^1/_4$-inch) notches at the center of the fold.

4. Fold the ends of the paper back toward the middle to create flaps.
5. Keeping the center folded, have your child hold the whistle with his first and second fingers in a V. This will control the airflow. The flaps should rest on the side of his face.
6. Blow. It will sound like an elephant in danger. If nothing happens, practice adjusting the tension in the fingers until the right amount of air is allowed through.

Bottle Bugle
Ages 4 and up

Have a blast learning about sound with this simple horn.

Gather
- Empty soda bottle or narrow-necked glass jar
- Water

Go
1. Give your child the bottle and show her how to blow across the opening to create a musical toot.
2. Ask your child what will happen to the sound if you add 2 inches or so of water to the bottle.
3. Do just that and listen for the results.

(For more sound fun, see "Common Senses" on page 37.)

Rice Rattle
Ages 4 and up

Add some shimmy to your child's summer with this easy-to-make instrument.

Gather
- Handfuls of rice, popcorn, or beans
- 2 paper or plastic cups the same size
- Packing tape

Go
1. Drop the rice into the cup.
2. Put the other cup rim to rim and secure the seal with packing tape.
3. Let your child shake, shake, shake.

Rump-pa-pa-pum Balloon Drum

Ages 6 and up

Kids will have a bang playing with this converted flowerpot.

Gather
- 6-inch diameter terra-cotta flowerpot
- Acrylic paints
- Large, good quality balloon
- 6 or so large rubber bands
- Dowels or sticks (optional)

Go
1. After setting up a clean work area with protective newspapers, let your child paint the pot. Let it dry completely.
2. Blow up the balloon to stretch it; let the air out.
3. Cut off the neck of the balloon. Stretch the balloon over the top the flowerpot until it stretches under the rim.
4. Secure the balloon with the rubber bands by wrapping them around the rim.
5. Your child is ready to beat the heat with his new drum.

Grow
Now "Make a joyful noise unto the Lord, all ye lands!" (Psalm 100:1, KJV)

ℭ   ℭ   ℭ

82

Watermelon Seed Wonders

Ages 4 and up

Use those little black beauties as artwork accents.

Gather
- Watermelon seeds
- Paper, cardboard, or poster board
- White glue
- Markers, crayons, or paints

Go
1. Let your children draw pictures on their paper with markers, crayons, or paints.
2. Help them decide where the picture needs black accents or texture. (Eyes, flower petals, borders, outlines, stripes, roof tiles, etc.)

3. Let older children glue the watermelon seeds where they will look good. Assist younger ones with this task.

Grow

Before the watermelon season is over, gather a handful of clean, dry seeds. Can you think of someone who would enjoy a "watermelon seed" picture? Perhaps a cold winter day might be the occasion to cheer up a neighbor or elderly person you know.

83

Car Pillow

Ages 4 and up
by Jenny Orndorff

Put the life back into a pair of worn-out jeans with this easy-to-make headrest.

Gather
- 1 pair old jeans
- 1 small package quilt stuffing
- 1 small package pillow stuffing
- 2 rubber bands
- 2 yards wide ribbon

Go

With supervision, even the youngest child can complete this project.
1. For each pillow, cut the leg off an old pair of jeans. You'll need a section about 18 to 22 inches long.
2. Estimate 5 inches from one edge and gather the fabric. Tie a rubber band around it.
3. Line the inside of the leg with quilt stuffing. This will help eliminate lumps.
4. Stuff it full with pillow stuffing.
5. Gather up the fabric at the loose end 5 inches down. Secure it with a rubber band.
6. Cut the ribbon in half, and tie a piece around each rubber band to make it look beautiful.

Grow

Know anyone taking a long car trip? This pillow would make a perfect gift because it doesn't take up much space and gives good neck support.

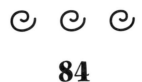

84

Potato Pots

Ages 4 and up

These portable gardens bring beauty to any windowsill.

Gather
- 2 large potatoes
- Soil from your backyard or planting mix
- Bird or grass seed
- Marbles or similar-sized rocks

Go
1. For younger kids, prepare the potatoes yourself. Let older kids scoop a large hole out of the center of each potato with a spoon or knife.
2. Let your child fill one potato hole with soil or planting mix.
3. Fill the other with marbles or similar-sized rocks.
4. Sprinkle the top of each potato with bird or grass seed.
5. Set the potatoes in a sunny place. Remind your child to water them every day.
6. The seeds in both potatoes will sprout in 7 to 10 days.
7. Make sure the grass is kept moist and compare the grass in the two potatoes in two weeks.

Grow
Read the parable of the sower found in Matthew 13:3-9, 18-23. Use the potato garden with the rocks as an example of the person whose faith didn't "take root."

85

Soap on a Rope

Ages 4 and up

Tie some fun into your summer with this squeaky clean idea.

Gather
- 1 to 2 bars of Dad's favorite soap
- Grater
- 3 tablespoons warm water

- Large mixing bowl
- Spoon or wooden stick
- 24 inches of decorative rope or heavy yarn

Go

1. Grate the soap until you have 2 cups.
2. Let your child mix the soap curlicues with the warm water.
3. The mixture should rest for 10 minutes.
4. While you are waiting, form a loop with the rope and knot the ends.
5. Help your child form the soap mixture into a ball and push the knot of the rope deep into the ball. Pack the soap firmly around it.
6. Hang your soap to dry. Allow two weeks for it to harden.

Grow

If you make this craft in the first week of June, it'll be ready for a Father's Day gift. Or you can include these special soaps in a gift bag for people in need. See pages 5-10 for more "People-Helping Projects."

ℯ   ℯ   ℯ

86

Terra-cotta Treasures

Ages 6 and up

Got a budding artist? Encourage that interest with this painting craft.

Gather

- Clay flowerpot, any size
- Acrylic paints
- Medium-sized paintbrushes
- Chalk

Go

1. Set up a work area with newspapers and make sure your child is wearing art aprons or old clothes. Acrylic paints stain.
2. Wash all the dust and dirt off the flowerpot.
3. Let your child draw pictures on the pot with the chalk.
4. When he is satisfied with the drawing, let him paint over the design.
5. Let the pot dry overnight.
6. Buy some flowers at the store or transplant something into the pot.

Grow

Wouldn't this make a great gift for a neighbor who needs cheering up?

ↄ ↄ ↄ

87

Parachute Pal

Ages 6 and up

Make this uplifting craft when your child has had a downer of a day.

Gather
- Kitchen trash bag, white if possible
- String
- Tape
- Bottle cork
- Scissors
- Ruler
- Acrylic paints

Go
1. Cut a 12-inch square from the plastic bag. Put a piece of tape on each corner.
2. After setting up a work area, have your child paint a design on the plastic square and a face on the cork. Let them dry.
3. Poke a hole through each piece of tape and thread a string through each hole. Tie knots in the strings.
4. Wrap a piece of string tightly around the cork. Attach the other strings to it.
5. Wrap a piece of tape around the string on the cork.
6. Let your child drop the parachute from a high place (safe for her and people below) or toss it up in the air.

Grow
Start a discussion by reading Psalm 145:14, "The LORD upholds all those who fall." Ask your child, "How is God like a parachute?" and "When has God helped our family in 'down' times?"

ℯ ℯ ℯ

88

Stick-to-It Basket

Ages 6 and up

A tisket, a tasket, a stick-and-twine basket.

Gather
- 28 sticks, each about 8 inches long
- Pliable branch about 14 inches long
- Twine
- Clear-drying glue
- Ribbons (optional)
- Wrapping paper (optional)

Go
Make sure the basket looks good and is sturdy.
1. Stack four sticks log-cabin style in a square. Tie the corners together with twine and secure with glue.
2. To make a base, tie and glue four more sticks—all in the same direction—across the bottom.
3. Add to the base by adding four more sticks crisscross (perpendicular) to the ones you just tied. Tie and glue them in place.
4. Build up the sides by making three more layers and securing them with twine and glue.
5. Bend the pliable branch over the basket and tie it to the top layer of sticks to make a handle.
6. Decorate it with a pretty ribbon and line it with decorative paper.

Grow
Fill this basket with good treats and let your child give it to a neighbor who is moving in. For recipe ideas, see pages 89-110.

89

Colonial Curlicues

Ages 8 and up

Turn thin strips of paper into brilliant decorations.

Gather
- 10 to 20 strips of construction paper ($1/8$-inch wide, 3 inches long), any color you want
- Toothpicks
- Clear-drying glue
- Waxed paper
- Colored cardboard (optional)

Go
You'll need to supervise the first two or three curlicues, then your child can be on her own.
1. Let her roll a strip of paper around the end of a toothpick.
2. With the other toothpick, she will dab a small amount of glue on the end of the strip and hold it until the glue dries.
3. Let her set this coil on the waxed paper (without the toothpick) and make another coil with a new strip of construction paper.
4. After she allows the coil to unravel a little, she should secure the end with glue.
5. Let her experiment with the coils by pinching one end or pinching both ends. Encourage her to make letters and other symbols.
6. After she has finished making different types of coils, she'll be ready to design her own patterns. Curlicues make great borders.
7. She should glue the coils to each other wherever they touch and let the glue dry overnight.
8. The next day, she can remove the pattern from the waxed paper and glue it on a piece of colored cardboard.
9. This colonial masterpiece, called "quilling," is ready to hang up or frame.

Grow
Now that she has the art of quilling mastered, ask her to design a symbol of faith or Christianity. Some common ones are a dove, cross, fish, or loaf of bread. Encourage her to give the picture to a non-Christian friend as a conversation starter about Jesus.

ℰ ℰ ℰ

90

Masks in the Making

Ages 7 and up
by Greta Wierenga

Papier-mâché a new face with newspapers and a milk jug.

Gather
- Poster paints or permanent markers
- 1 plastic gallon-sized jug (a distilled water container or milk jug)
- Newspapers
- Wallpaper paste or white glue
- Piece of elastic about 6 inches long or a craft stick
- Construction paper (optional)
- Pipe cleaners (optional)

Go
1. Let your child tear the newspapers into 6-inch long and 1-inch wide strips.
2. Cut the plastic jug in half from top to bottom. Pick one half for a mold.
3. Cut eye holes about an inch from the top.
4. Let your child brush a layer of glue or paste over the outside of the jug. Then he will lay newspaper strips on the glue. Make sure he doesn't cover the eye holes.
5. Let him add one more layer of glue and newspapers.
6. It should dry overnight.
7. Add two layers of glue and newspapers per day until there are six or eight layers on.
8. When the newspapers and glue have dried thoroughly, carefully pull the plastic away from the newspapers.
9. Your child is ready to paint or color the mask anyway he likes.
10. Glue on ears, whiskers, etc., made with the construction paper and pipe cleaners.
11. Staple the piece of elastic to the sides to keep the mask on or glue a craft stick to the bottom center as a handle.

Grow
Ask your child why he chose the mask he did. Discuss the concept of "masking" feelings. If appropriate, share a story from your life when you felt one way and acted another way. Ask your child if he thinks God was fooled by your "mask." Continue the discussion until your child knows that while a person can fool other people with a "mask," God knows and cares about each person's true feelings.

ℯ   ℯ   ℯ

91

Coin Collectors

Make-your-own containers will help you save your coins.

Piggy Pals

Ages 4 and up
by Christine Kuizema

Plastic bottles and some craft scraps create a see-through, see-you-through savings bank.

Gather
- 1 bottle (water-bottle style) with cap
- 4 large cotton balls or pom-poms
- 2 small pink cotton balls or pom-poms
- 2 triangles of pink felt
- 2 plastic google eyes
- 1 pink pipe cleaner
- Glue

Go
1. Cut a 2-inch slot in the side of the bottle.
2. Let your child glue four large cotton balls on the opposite side of the slot.
3. Ask her to wrap the piece of pipe cleaner around a pencil to make it curly.
4. With a sharp pin, poke a hole in the bottom of the bottle and let your child stick a small part of the pipe cleaner in the hole.
5. Have her glue two plastic eyes on each side of the bottle cap.
6. For ears, let her glue two pink triangles to the bottleneck just above the eyes.
7. She should also glue two small pink cotton balls onto the bottle cap to make a snout.

Tennis Ball Treasury

Ages 6 and up

Saving money can be a ball with this change bank.

Gather
- Clean tennis ball
- Craft knife

- Glue
- Buttons or google eyes
- Yarn
- Acrylic paints or markers
- Paint brushes

Go

1. Cut a 2-inch slot in the tennis ball, at right angles to the seams.
2. Imagining that the slit is the center top of the head, your child can glue on a button or google eyes. Let dry.
3. Let your child draw or paint on a mouth.
4. Help him to use yarn to create a hairdo. Braids, long locks, or a crew cut work well.
5. Using lots of glue, help him secure the hair to the ball.
6. Prop the ball up so the glue can dry.
7. Show him how to squeeze the ball so the slot opens and he can push in coins.

Grow

If your child makes three banks, it will be simple to teach him money management. One bank is for saving to give to the church and people in need. The second bottle is for your child's long-term savings. The third is for spending right now.

ⓔ ⓔ ⓔ

92

Butterfly Fan

Ages 4 and up

Just paint and fold to create these delicate wings.

Gather

- Art paper (you need a heavier and more absorbent paper than school or computer stock)
- Paintbrush
- Scissors
- Twist tie or pipe cleaner
- Cup of water
- Watercolor paints
- Ruler

Go

1. Let your child paint a small section of the paper with water.

2. She should then dip her brush in some paint and dab the paper. The paint will burst out in color as it mixes with the water.
3. Let her experiment with different colors until the whole paper is swirled in bright color. By keeping the brush clean in between dippings, she will get the truest colors.
4. When the paper is dry, help her cut it into a 5-inch square and a 4-inch square.
5. Show her how to fold each square "accordion"-style by bending a small piece of the corner ($^1/_4$ to $^1/_3$ of an inch), turning over the paper and folding the same amount. She will keep turning and folding the paper until the whole piece of paper is folded.
6. Stack the bigger piece of paper on the smaller one, and pinch them together in the middle. Use the twist tie to fasten them together. Bend the rest of the twist tie to make it look like antennae.
7. Hang the butterfly from the ceiling or create several more and make a mobile.

Grow

Butterflies are a symbol of a new creation or new life because they turn from a land-loving caterpillar into a beautiful winged insect. Ask your child how knowing Jesus can change a person from the inside out. How does Jesus make a person beautiful? See 2 Corinthians 5:17, "Therefore, if anyone is in Christ, he is a new creation; the old has gone, the new has come!"

ℰ   ℰ   ℰ

93

Jar Gems

Ages 6 and up
by Marianne K. Hering

Transform a mason jar into a masterpiece.

Gather
- Buttons and beads
- Mason jar with a two-piece lid
- 8-inch circle of tulle
- White craft glue

Go
1. Let your child glue the buttons or beads on top of the flat part of the jar lid. Leave about $^1/_4$ inch around the edge plain.
2. Help your child put the flat part of the lid on the jar. Place the tulle circle on top—be sure it's centered.
3. Glue it in place.

4. Screw on the ring part of the lid.

5. Use the jar as a container for candy, nuts, or other gifts.

Grow

You can make this a "Treasures in Heaven" jar. Fill the jar with candy. Each time your child helps you without being asked, write that good deed down on a piece of paper and put it in the jar—and give him a piece of candy. When it's full, read the slips of paper together.

ℰ ℰ ℰ

94

Sticky Business

Ages 4 and up

Stuck on stickers? Here's how your child can make his own.

Gather
- Magazines or catalogs with glossy pages
- Scissors
- Newspaper
- 2 teaspoons water
- 1 tablespoon flavored gelatin
- Coffee mug
- Spoon
- Small paintbrush

Go
1. Give your child a pile of magazines you no longer want. Let him cut out some fun pictures. Help him lay them face down on the newspaper.
2. Put the water and gelatin in the mug and stir. Place the mug in the microwave and heat for one minute or until the water boils. Stir again until gelatin dissolves.
3. Let the mixture cool down. With the liquid still warm, let your child use the paintbrush to evenly coat the back of each picture.
4. Let the pictures dry for two days. They will curl up as they dry.
5. When your child is ready to use the stickers, let him lick the back. He will get a sweet-tasting lick every time he sticks one on an envelope, letter, or notebook.

Grow

These stickers look great on stationery. Encourage your kids to write a letter to their grandparents and decorate it with stickers.

ϱ ϱ ϱ

95

Summer Shake-Up

Ages 4 and up

This mini meteor exhibit will shower excitement on the dullest of days.

Gather
- Small, clean jar with a screw-on lid
- Waterproof glue or caulking (White glue won't do; your best bet is clear caulking from a hardware store.)
- Small plastic toys (house, people, animals)
- Silver glitter; or red, white, and blue glitter
- Water

Go
Young children will need supervision. Older children can do it alone.
1. Glue the plastic toys to the bottom of the lid. (Let the glue dry completely or the figures may float away one day!)
2. Pour the glitter into the jar. You need at least enough to cover the bottom. (If you want a Fourth of July fireworks display, use red, white, and blue glitter.)
3. Fill the jar to the top with water. Then screw on the lid tightly.
4. Spread the waterproof glue or caulking around the outside edge of the lid to keep the jar from leaking. Let it dry for at least one day.
5. Let your child give the jar a good shake, set it on the lid and watch the meteors fall.

Grow
For more on star gazing and God, see "Star Search" on page 49.

ↄ   ↄ   ↄ

96

Handy Dandy Apron

Ages 4 and up

This cute kitchen coverall is perfect for helping hands.

Gather

For each apron:

- White "flour sack" dishcloth, about 22 by 38 inches
- 6 feet of cording or thick ribbon
- Newspaper
- Brightly colored fabric paints or acrylic paints
- Tube fabric paints for writing
- Pie pan or other disposable container
- Sewing needle and white thread

Go

You sew the apron; the children can decorate it with their handprints.

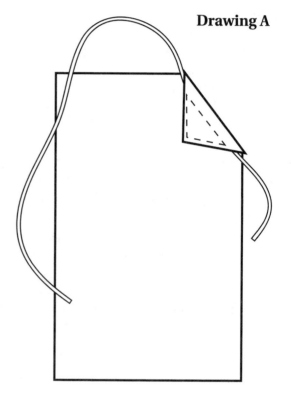

Drawing A

1. Hold the dishcloth vertically to your child's shoulder. Mark where the dishcloth hits his or her knee.
2. At the mark, fold over the extra cloth. The fold is now the top of the apron.
3. Lay the cording on the apron, as shown in drawing A.
4. Fold the top corners down, leaving 5 inches open at the center.
5. Sew the folded corners down and the rest of the triangle down, otherwise it will flap open.
6. Adjust the neck loop so that it fits over your child's head; make sure the waist ties are equal lengths.
7. Secure the cording by sewing it down at the four corners, as shown in drawing B.
8. Cover a work area with newspapers. Pour the darkest paint into the pie pan, following the instructions on the paint container.

9. Have your child dip his or her hands into the paint. Blot them lightly on a newspaper and then press them firmly on the front of the apron.
10. When you are finished with that color, wash your child's hands. Get another pie pan and repeat step 9. Continue until the apron is covered with handprints. (You may want to make One-of-a Kind Critters on page 113 while you're at it.)
11. Let dry.
12. With the tube paint, finish the apron by writing this verse on it: When you eat the labor of your hands, you shall be happy (Psalm 128:2, NCV).

Drawing B

Grow

Discuss the meaning of "When you eat the labor of your hands, You shall be happy." Explain what "the labor of your hands" is to your child and get him to expand the concept beyond food or other tangible items. (What is the work of doctors, teachers, and mothers, for example?) Ask why the Bible says people who work for their money, food, and housing are happy.

ℰ   ℰ   ℰ

97

High-Flying Fun

Soar to new heights with these two wind crafts.

Kite Made for Flight

Ages 8 and up

This plastic-bag kite will help your children experience the value of following God's lead.

Gather
- Plastic trashcan bag, 13-gallon tall kitchen size or larger (the thicker the bag, the sturdier the kite)
- Marking pen

- Acrylic paints
- Paint brushes
- Two dowels, $^1/_8$-inch thick and 16 inches long
- Masking tape
- Measuring tape or yardstick
- Scissors
- Kite string
- Crepe paper

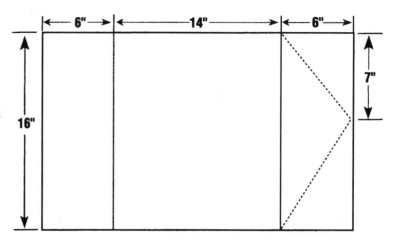

Go

Most children will need you to make the kite for them. If you need a simpler version, see "Wind Bag" below.

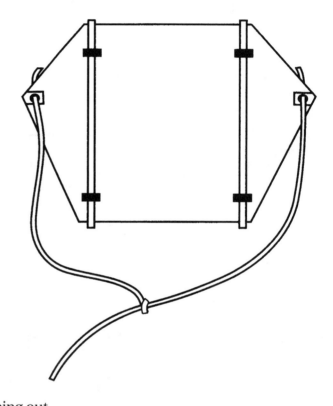

1. Cut the plastic bag into a rectangle 26-by-16 inches. Using the marking pen and scissors, measure and trim sides as shown.
2. Let your children paint a design on the plastic and let it dry. (Watch out! Acrylic paints will stain fabric and carpets.)
3. Tape the two dowels from top to bottom, 6 inches in from each side, as shown.
4. Put tape on the two side corners. Punch a small hole in each piece of tape.
5. Cut a piece of string 40 inches long for the bridle. Thread it through the holes and tie a big knot in each end to keep the string from slipping out.
6. Attach the flying string to the center of the bridle.
7. Your child can tape pieces of crepe paper to the bottom of the kite for a tail.
8. Older kids can launch their own kites. You'll have to help younger children get the kite in the wind and then let them hold the string. Here are some tips how:
9. To fly the kite, find out which way the wind is blowing by holding the kite in your hand and watching the direction it moves.
10. Walk into the wind to get your kite in the air, letting out more string as you go.
11. If it starts to wobble, pull in the string a bit until it's steady.
12. When you are ready to stop, cut the string and watch what happens to the kite.

Wind Bag

Ages 4 and up
by Lauren Galinsky

This brown-bag craft is a breeze to make.

Gather
- Small paper bag
- Crayons or markers
- Glitter, jewels, sequins (optional)
- Glue (optional)
- Invisible tape
- Hole punch
- Kite string

Go
1. Let your child decorate both sides of the bag with crayons and glitter.
2. Help him put a piece of tape on the bottom corners of one side of the bag.
3. He can punch a hole through the tape on each corner.
4. Cut two pieces of kite string. Each piece should be about 12 inches long.
5. Put a piece through one of the holes and tie a knot. Do the same to the other side. Tie the loose ends of the string together.
6. Attach the roll of kite string to both strings, and your child is ready to fly.

Grow
Make sure your children understand that kites fly because of the wind and the string. Ask them what happens when a kite's string is cut. (It falls.) Kites look as if they are really free, soaring. But in reality, it is the tug of the string that keeps it aloft. Ask your children what will happen if they "cut" themselves off from God's guidance.

℮   ℮   ℮

98

Blueprint Beauties

Ages 4 and up

With special paper and the sun's help, your kids can create extraordinary designs.

Gather
- Blueprint paper from an office supply store
- Leaves, flowers, sticks, and other outdoor items with interesting shapes

- Large board
- Tape

Go

1. Tape the blueprint paper to the board.
2. Let your child arrange the leaves, flowers, and sticks on the paper in a pretty design.
3. Place the board outside in the sun for about five minutes.
4. Ask your child to remove the objects from the paper to see the design.
5. Let your children experiment with more blueprint paper and household items.

Grow

You can use this technique to make decorative Bible verses. Using toothpicks, rubber bands, or paper clips, spell out "God is light." After the light does its job, remove the objects and tack the paper up somewhere visible as a reminder of His power.

ℰ ℰ ℰ

99

For the Birds

Ages 4 and up
by Ashley Thomas

A milk jug and some birdseed make elegant dining for your family's fine-feathered friends.

Gather

- 1 plastic gallon-sized milk jug
- Jar lid approximately 3 inches in diameter
- Marking pen
- Sharp craft knife
- 2 sticks or short pieces of dowel
- 2 yards strong twine or fishing line
- Birdseed

Go

1. Ask your child to rinse out the milk carton.
2. Using the jar lid as a guide, let your child draw circles on the two large panels that don't connect to the handle.
3. Cut out the holes with the craft knife.
4. Poke small holes underneath the larger holes.
5. Let your child put a stick or dowel through each hole to create the perch.

6. Poke two very small holes near the top opening of the jug. Make each hole on opposite sides of the jug.
7. Thread the twine or fishing line through the holes. Tie a slip-proof knot at the top, leaving enough twine to hang the bird feeder.
8. As a family discuss the best place to hang the bird feeder and put it out for your new friends.

Grow

As you and your children watch the birds eat from your bird feeder, talk about the ways that God cares for your needs.

100

Fruit-Filled Fun

Ages 4 and up

Grow an apple inside a glass bottle? Here's how.

Gather
- Fruit tree with blossoms or the tiny beginnings of fruit
- Clear, small-necked bottle
- Paper
- Waterproof tape

Go

1. On a small piece of paper, write or let your child write this: "Made in (your city) by God." Help her bend the paper just a little and slip it into the bottle. If the message can be read through the bottle, it is in correctly. If not, fiddle with the paper until the words are readable.
2. Slip the neck of the bottle over a tiny, healthy looking sprout of budding fruit.
3. Tape it to the branch in any way feasible to keep the bottle in place.
4. Ask your child to check the fruit often to see how it is growing.
5. When the fruit is nearly full-grown, clip the branch near the top of the bottle.

Grow

Let your child show the fruit to your friends and family. They will marvel at the fruit and the message—God is a great Creator!

℮   ℮   ℮

101

Chalk It Up

Ages 4 and up

Mix your own sidewalk crayons out of soap flakes and food coloring.

Gather
- $1/_8$ cup water
- $7/_8$ cup soap flakes
- Food coloring
- Plastic ice cube tray

Go
1. Pour the water into a mixing bowl. Add the soap flakes and stir the mixture until all the lumps are gone.
2. Add a few drops of one food coloring to the soap mixture. Stir it until the color is even.
3. Press spoonfuls of the soap mixture into the ice cube tray. Fill each hole completely.
4. Start again with another cup of soapflakes, using a different food coloring. Keep repeating the steps until the ice cube tray is full.
5. Let your soap cubes dry in a warm place for a few days. Test to make sure the soap is hard by pressing with your finger.
6. Pop the soap crayons out of the tray. Your child can use them to color on the sidewalk. When he's finished drawing, the pictures will wash away.

Grow
Let little hands use these crayons to practice handwriting. Print a short Bible verse on the sidewalk and let your child draw over the letters.

FOCUS ON THE FAMILY®

Welcome to the Family!

Whether you received this book as a gift, borrowed it from
a friend, or purchased it yourself, we're glad you read it! It's just
one of the many helpful, insightful, and encouraging
resources produced by Focus on the Family.

In fact, that's what Focus on the Family is all about—providing inspira-
tion, information, and biblically based advice to people in all stages of life.

It began in 1977 with the vision of one man, Dr. James Dobson, a licensed
psychologist and author of 16 best-selling books on marriage, parenting,
and family. Alarmed by the societal, political, and economic pressures
that were threatening the existence of the American family, Dr. Dobson
founded Focus on the Family with one employee—an assistant—
and a once-a-week radio broadcast, aired on only 36 stations.

Now an international organization, Focus on the Family is dedicated
to preserving Judeo-Christian values and strengthening the family
through more than 70 different ministries, including eight separate
daily radio broadcasts; television public service announcements;
13 publications; and a steady series of books and award-winning
films and videos for people of all ages and interests.

Recognizing the needs of, as well as the sacrifices and important
contribution made by, such diverse groups as educators, physicians,
attorneys, crisis pregnancy center staff, and single parents,
Focus on the Family offers specific outreaches to uphold and
minister to these individuals, too. And it's all done for one purpose,
and one purpose only: to encourage and strengthen individuals
and families through the life-changing message of Jesus Christ.

• • •

For more information about the ministry, or if we can be of help to your
family, simply write to Focus on the Family, Colorado Springs, CO 80995
or call 1-800-A-FAMILY (1-800-232-6459). Friends in Canada may write
Focus on the Family, P.O. Box 9800, Stn. Terminal, Vancouver, B.C. V6B 4G3
or call 1-800-661-9800. Visit our Web site—www.family.org—
to learn more about Focus on the Family or to find out if
there is an associate office in your country.

We'd love to hear from you!

Try These Other Faith-Strengthening Resources
From Focus on the Family®

Family Nights Tool Chest

Heritage Builders "Family Nights Tool Chest" series offers creative, interactive ways to teach biblical principles to children in fun, memorable ways. Designed for parents to use as part of their own "Family Nights," these activities will help plant biblical truths deep in the hearts and minds of children.

Mealtime Moments

Make your family's time around the dinner table meaningful with *Mealtime Moments,* a book that brings you great discussion starters and activities for teaching your children about your faith. Kids will have fun getting involved with games, trivia questions, and theme nights, all based on spiritually sound ideas. Perfect for the whole family! Spiralbound.

Bedtime Blessings

Strengthen the precious bond between you, your child, and God by making *Bedtime Blessings* a special part of your evenings together. From best-selling author John Trent, Ph.D., and Heritage Builders, this book is filled with stories, activities, and blessing prayers to help you practice the biblical model of "blessing."

Joy Ride!

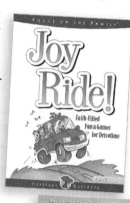

Use your drive time to teach your kids how faith can be part of everyday life with *Joy Ride!* A wonderful resource for parents, this book features activities, puzzles, games, and discussion starters to help get your kids thinking about—and living out—what they believe.

The Last Days of Eugene Meltsner

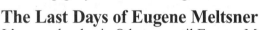

It's a regular day in Odyssey until Eugene Meltsner hops into Whit's new invention, the Micro-Simulator, intent on a voyage of self-discovery. But along the way, he finds himself in the middle of a bank heist and a burning building! Kids ages 6 and up will love the first installment in an all-new Adventures in Odyssey video series, and learn action-packed lessons about trusting God and living each day to the fullest. Video and paperback.

The Big Picture

Adventures in Odyssey fans—or anyone ages 8 and up—are sure to love *The Big Picture.* In addition to stories about Novacom—the big company that comes to town when the Timothy Center gets into financial trouble—the audio album is filled with episodes that teach important lessons on: faith in action, choosing friends, prayer, obedience, and much more.

Clubhouse Jr. Magazine

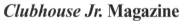

Clubhouse Jr. is Focus on the Family's monthly magazine that's perfect for kids ages 4 to 8. Each issue is filled with fun crafts, games, tales, and more—all emphasizing scriptural principles.

Clubhouse Magazine

Focus on the Family's *Clubhouse* magazine is sure to delight children ages 8 to 12 with exciting puzzles, activities, and faith-building stories.

• • •

Look for these special books in your Christian bookstore or request a copy by calling 1-800-A-FAMILY (1-800-232-6459). Friends in Canada may write Focus on the Family, P.O. Box 9800, Stn. Terminal, Vancouver, B.C. V6B 4G3 or call 1-800-661-9800.

Visit our Web site (www.family.org) to learn more about the ministry or find out if there is a Focus on the Family office in your country.